Eggs & Cheese

DAVID & CHARLES

Newton Abbot London

British Library Cataloguing in Publication Data
Eggs & cheese.—(David & Charles Kitchen Workshop)
  1. Cookery (Eggs)   2. Cookery (Cheese)
  I. Egg og osteretter. *English*
  641.6'75   TX745

ISBN 0-7153-8455-4

© Illustrations: A/S Hjemmet 1980
  Text: David & Charles 1983

Filmset by MS Filmsetting Ltd, Frome, Somerset
and printed in The Netherlands
by Smeets Offset BV, Weert
for David & Charles (Publishers) Limited
Brunel House, Newton Abbot, Devon

Eggs and cheese are both excellent foods which are often used unimaginatively. This book has many recipes for egg and cheese dishes which introduce a wide and exciting new range of possibilities.

What You Should Know About Eggs

Few foods are as useful and diverse as eggs. They can be a complete meal or course by themselves – boiled, fried, poached, scrambled or as omelettes – or they can be a major constituent of many other dishes. Eggs are binding agents, helping pancakes, omelettes and soufflés to hold together better; stiffly beaten egg-whites or egg-yolks and sugar beaten together act as a raising agent in baking or in soufflés, for instance; whole eggs or yolks are used to thicken soups and sauces; and beaten egg brushed over pastry or breads before baking glazes the food, giving a nice, brown shiny surface. Most important of all, eggs have great nutritional value and contain both minerals and vitamins.

EGG TIPS
Fresh eggs should have a clean, whole shell, a thick, jelly-like white, and a golden yolk in the centre.

To test for freshness There is an air chamber at the blunt end of the egg which increases in size as an egg deteriorates, through age or bad storage.
Put a raw egg in a glass of cold water. If fresh, the egg will lie on the bottom; if less than fresh, the blunt end will rise; if stale or bad, the egg

will float. Always break an egg into a saucer first to double-check.

Egg storage All eggs should be stored in a cool place or in the refrigerator, pointed end downwards. This means that the yolk rests on the white instead of against the air chamber or the shell, and thus lasts longer.
Egg shells are porous, so they should never be stored next to strong-smelling foods.

Egg freezing Whole eggs cannot be frozen, but yolks and whites can be frozen separately or beaten well together.

Boiled or raw? If you have hard-boiled eggs in the refrigerator with raw eggs, 'spin' the egg on a surface to see whether it is cooked or raw. If hard-boiled, the egg will spin fast; if raw, it will spin slowly.

Egg sizes Shop-bought eggs are sold in packages of 6 or occasionally 10. They used to be labelled Large, Standard, Medium or Small, and are now, following adoption of the EEC sizing system, numbered from 1–7. Most recipes require Standard eggs – Sizes 3 or 4 – while Large eggs are sizes 1 or 2, Medium are size 5, and Small are 6 or even 7.

White or brown? There is no difference at all between white and brown eggs. In France and Britain, brown eggs are thought to be tastier and healthier; in America white eggs are thought to be more pure, and are more popular. What *does* make a difference, though – in the nutritive value and in the taste – is the feed given to the laying hens. Battery hens can, for example, be fed too much fish- or bone-meal, which can affect the taste of their eggs.

Over-boiled eggs Eggs boiled too long get an unsightly dark rim at the edge of the yolk. These can be used in a salad. Mix chopped egg and mayonnaise, and stir in some freshly-chopped herbs, seasoning and a little lemon juice.

Slicing eggs Eggs to be sliced or halved should not be too large, as the white and the yolk tend to fall apart.

Egg shells Egg-shells can be used as a bleaching agent for cloth. Rinse the shells well, dry them, and crush to a powder. Put the powder in a little cloth bag and add it to whites that are to be boiled or washed at a very high temperature.
Egg-shells are also used in consommé and cleared jellies, because the impurities cling to them.

How to separate eggs
1 Knock the egg against the edge of a bowl or table.
2 Over a bowl, put your thumb inside the shell.
3 Separate the two halves of shell.
4 Keep the yolk in one half shell, and let the white run down into the bowl.
5 Pour the yolk into the other half shell to get out the remaining white. It is easiest to use a special yolk-white divider, or even an ordinary funnel. Break the egg into the funnel and let the white run down into a glass. The yolk will then be left whole in the top of the funnel.

Left-over yolks or whites Use up yolks straightaway in a custard – baked, boiled or caramel; as a glaze; for an egg and breadcrumb coating; for binding a mixture, like fish cakes or beefburgers; in a mayonnaise or hollandaise sauce; to enrich creamed potatoes or a shortcrust pastry. Yolks will add to the taste and texture of whatever you make. Use up whites by making meringues or creamy dessert mixtures. Meringues are made of stiffly beaten egg-whites and sugar. If you want a fluffy, porous consistency for small meringue shapes, for instance, use the first recipe (called meringue suisse). If you want a more compact meringue, to last longer, as a base for fruit or icecream, choose the second recipe (for meringue cuite).

Meringues should be baked in the middle of the oven to begin with, and then at the foot of the oven. They should always be baked in a preheated oven at its lowest setting (110–120°C, 225–250°F, Gas $\frac{1}{4}$–$\frac{1}{2}$). If meringues start to brown, turn the heat down even lower, or prop the oven door open with a wooden spoon. Depending on size, the meringues should be ready after 2–4 hours, when they feel firm and dry, and lift easily from the baking paper or tray.

Meringues I
3 egg whites
175g (6oz) sugar

Pour the egg whites into a clean, dry bowl. Beat with a whisk or electric mixer until the whites hold stiff peaks. Add $\frac{1}{3}$ of the sugar, and beat again until the mixture has become a firm, compact foam. Fold in the remaining sugar, very carefully, a few tablespoons at a time.

Meringues II
3 egg whites
175g (6oz) icing sugar

Put the egg whites and sugar into a clean, dry bowl and place the bowl over a saucepan with a little water in it. (The bowl must be slightly larger than the saucepan so that the steam from the water doesn't rise and

Fresh, newly-laid eggs. Use them on their own – fried, boiled, poached – or as a good and inexpensive ingredient in many dishes.

escape.) The water must simmer only. Beat the mixture thoroughly until it is firm (take a tablespoon of mixture from the bowl and see if it holds its shape).

Troll Cream
Use 25g (1oz) sugar to each egg white.
Beat the sugar and egg whites

together and stir in fresh cranberries, defrosted frozen ones, or cranberry jam. Other berries or jam could be substituted.

Dessert Cream
Mix stiffly whipped cream with stiffly beaten egg whites for a delicious fluffy cream with greater volume and fewer calories.

What You Should Know About Cheese

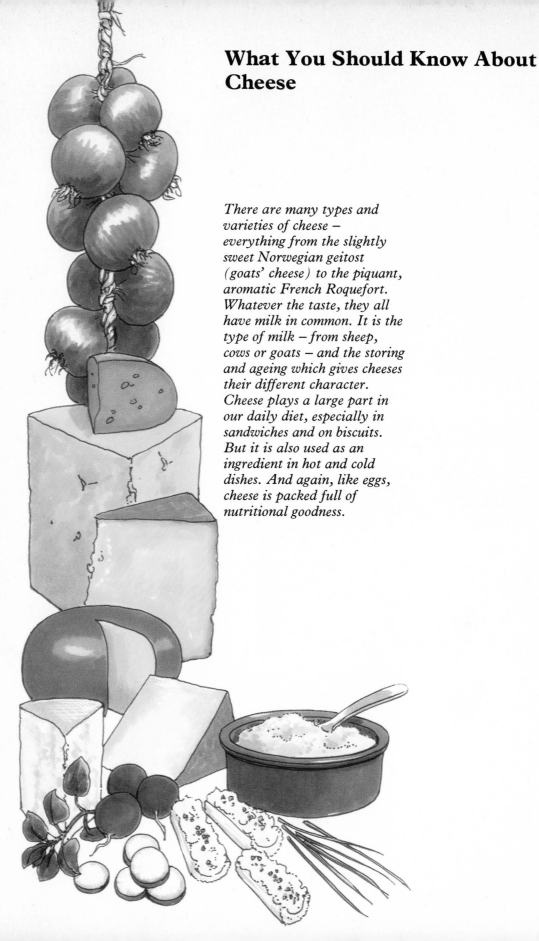

There are many types and
varieties of cheese –
everything from the slightly
sweet Norwegian geitost
(goats' cheese) to the piquant,
aromatic French Roquefort.
Whatever the taste, they all
have milk in common. It is the
type of milk – from sheep,
cows or goats – and the storing
and ageing which gives cheeses
their different character.
Cheese plays a large part in
our daily diet, especially in
sandwiches and on biscuits.
But it is also used as an
ingredient in hot and cold
dishes. And again, like eggs,
cheese is packed full of
nutritional goodness.

CHEESE TIPS

● Cheese *can* keep well, but it is best to buy small quantities at a time to ensure that you always eat it at its best.

● When buying cheese, look carefully at it first. Avoid anything which looks too dry, too hard, too soft and, if pre-packed, as if it had 'sweated'.

● All kinds of cheese should be kept in a cool larder, or in the refrigerator. Store in a plastic container preferably, but it can be wrapped in clingfilm or foil.

● Never serve hard or soft cheeses straight from the refrigerator. Take them from the refrigerator at least 1 hour before serving, and allow to come to room temperature.

● All cheese must be either tightly wrapped or carefully covered, and never leave it too near other food which has a strong taste or smell.

How to Use Cheese

Cheese may be served at almost any time of day (on the Continent it is often eaten at breakfast). For most of us, however, cheese is vital for an instant snack, as a major constituent of a ploughman's lunch – served with crusty French bread, butter and salad – or as a tasty finale to a good dinner, accompanied by biscuits, perhaps some crisp celery stalks, and the red wine which is cheese's natural partner. And a cheese and wine party is still an enjoyable – and fairly economical – way of entertaining.

But cheese is also used in cooked dishes – in sauces, soufflés, with bread for Welsh Rarebit or toasted sandwiches, in savoury scones, pies and pastry, and as a topping for many dishes which are to be oven-baked.

Types of Cheese:

There is now a large variety of cheeses available, from all over the world. The following is a basic selection of some of the better-known.

Hard and semi-hard cheeses

Gouda originates from the town of Gouda in Holland, but is now produced in many other countries. It has a high butter-fat content, and is golden-yellow in colour. Creamy tasting, it should not be used for cooking.

Edam is now produced in many countries but was first made in the Dutch town of Edam. The cheese is round, and always encased in a red wax rind. In taste it is rather similar to Gouda but Gouda is made from whole milk, while Edam is made from partly skimmed milk. Do not use in cooking.

Jarlsberg is a cheese from Norway which is becoming increasingly popular elsewhere. It is a rich cheese with large holes and a slightly sweet flavour.

Emmenthal cheese came originally from Switzerland, but is now made elsewhere as well. It is dull yellow in colour, with cherry-sized holes, and has a sweetish, nutty flavour that grows fuller with age.

Gruyère is another Swiss-French cheese, higher in butterfat than Emmenthal, and has smaller holes and a sharper taste. Both are delicious as eating and as cooking cheese – the latter in the famous Swiss fondues particularly.

Cheddar is almost certainly the most popular of all English cheeses. Although indisputably English by its name, it is now made all over the world: there are Scottish, New Zealand, Irish, Australian and Canadian Cheddars on the market. Its full, nutty flavour, ranging from mild to very strong, makes it an all-purpose cheese, but especially suitable for cooking.

Leicester is a mild English cheese, recognisable by its red colour and its flaky texture. Good for cooking, but it dries out easily.

Lancashire is a crumbly, off-white English cheese which is good for cooking because of its high fat content.

Parmesan is probably the best-known Italian hard cheese. Off-white inside its dark rind, it is strong and fragrant, and excellent for cooking. It is expensive to buy by the piece, but if used for grating over foods, in the Italian manner, it lasts a long time. It is also available ready grated. In Italy, it is sold according to its age, and the oldest 'Parmigiani' are the most expensive and popular.

Port-Salut was first made by the Trappist monks in France, and is now produced in many other countries. It is a semi-hard, yellow cheese with a reddish rind, and a bland taste which gets stronger as it ripens.

Soft and cream cheeses

Cottage cheese is made from the curds of skimmed milk, and is low in calories, therefore popular with weight-watchers. It is available with many added flavourings such as onion and pineapple.

Boursin (also known as Boursault) is a French cream cheese with herb, pepper or garlic flavouring.

Feta is a semi-soft curd cheese from Greece. It is made from sheeps' milk, and is very salty. It is used mainly in salads.

Mozzarella is a curd cheese from Italy, used in salads, as a topping for pizzas, and deep-fried in a bread-crumb coating for the delicious appetiser, Mozzarella in Carrozza.

Brie is known as 'le roi des fromages' (the king of cheeses). It is large and round, about 7.5cm (3in) thick with a pale yellow inside and a white rind. The flavour is mild, and is best when cut from a whole cheese. Brie is made from cows' milk, and is fully ripe when the cheese bulges rather than runs when the surface is pressed. Always serve at room temperature.

Camembert resembles Brie, and is made from cows' milk as well, but is lighter in colour, and has a stronger flavour. It is available whole in boxes, or in individually wrapped portions. The ripeness test is the same as for Brie; and if it is over-ripe it will smell of ammonia and taste sour.

Goats' milk cheeses

Pur-chèvre and *Mi-chèvre* are the names given to the white French goat cheeses. Some are quite firm, others are soft. In France a distinction is made between Pur-chèvre, which is made of goats' milk alone, and Mi-chèvre, which is made of both goats' and cows' milk.

Goat cheeses have become popular over the last decade or so, and are now increasingly made in the United Kingdom.

Ekte geitost (genuine goats' cheese) is a brown, Norwegian cheese with a slightly sweet flavour. It is made from the whey of goats' milk. It has a firm, but at the same time soft, consistency.

Blandet geitost (mixed goats' cheese) is made from a mixture of goats' and cows' milk. It is milder in flavour

than the genuine ekte geitost.

Blue cheeses

Stilton is the king of cheeses for the English. The surface is brown and uneven, inside it is a rich creamy colour, veined with blue mould. It is crumbly, difficult to cut, with a strong, tangy taste (it is commonly sold in jars, and taken out with a spoon). Soaking it in port – a traditional and popular way of eating Stilton – masks its flavour somewhat, but eaten on biscuits with an accompanying glass of port, it is truly delicious.

Danish Blue cheese is white with blue veins, and is made from milk with a high cream content. It has a soft, slightly crumbly texture. Its

strong salty flavour diminishes as the cheese matures.

Roquefort is the best-known French blue cheese. It is made from sheeps' milk curds, and ripened in limestone caves near the town of Roquefort. The cheese is soft, pale cream in colour, with the characteristic blue-green veins. Roquefort has a soft, crumbly consistency and a strong salty flavour.

Gorgonzola is one of the best-known Italian cheeses. It is creamy-white in colour with blue-green marbling. It has a sharp, aromatic smell and flavour.

Dolcelatte is another veined Italian cheese, whitish in colour with blue-green veins throughout. It is soft in texture with a full flavour.

Boiled Eggs

An egg that is to be boiled should be newly laid, without any cracks and not too cold (take the eggs out of the refrigerator some time before you intend to boil them).

Pierce the blunt end of the egg with a needle or a special egg-pricker. This lets the air from the air chamber escape, and will prevent the egg cracking during boiling. Fill a saucepan with plenty of water, bring to a boil and then take it off the heat while you put the eggs carefully into the water. Use a large spoon and put in one egg at a time, or put all the eggs into a steel basket and lower the basket into the water. Place the saucepan back on the heat immediately and allow the eggs to cook.

Cooking time – soft-boiled eggs

Small eggs .... 3 min
Standard eggs .... 3½ min
Large eggs .... 4–4½ min

Cooking time – hard-boiled eggs

The cooking time here depends on how you like your egg yolks. Some like the yolks to be completely dry, while others prefer them slightly soft.

Small eggs .... 6–9 min
Standard eggs .... 9–10 min
Large eggs .... 10–12 min

Poached Eggs

Poached eggs are eggs cooked in water without their shells. The eggs *must* be fresh to get the best results. Let your water come to a boil and add 1 × 5ml tsp (1tsp) salt per litre (1¾pt) water. A little vinegar may be added to the boiling water to make sure that the whites will be firm, but this should not be necessary if the eggs are completely fresh. Pour one egg at a time into a cup and let it slip carefully into the boiling water. Collect the white around the yolk with a tablespoon. The eggs should simmer, but not boil for 3–4 min. Lift the eggs out with a slotted spoon and put them into cold or hot water according to how you intend to use them.

Poached eggs may be used in a variety of ways – in soups, in sauces, in creamed dishes, and on toast for breakfast.

Poached Eggs in Curry Sauce
(right)
(serves 4)

8 eggs
For the sauce :
15g (½oz) butter
1 onion, chopped
1 × 15ml tbsp (1tbsp) flour
½–1 × 15ml tbsp (½–1tbsp) curry powder
275ml (½pt) chicken stock
¼ × 5ml tsp (¼tsp) salt
1 small can mushrooms, drained
100g (4oz) cooked ham, cubed

1 Poach the eggs and keep warm.
2 Melt the butter, add chopped onion and sauté until golden. Sprinkle with flour and curry powder and sauté for a few more minutes.
3 Add the stock gradually. Season with salt and cook for 5 min. Slice the drained mushrooms and add to the sauce, along with the cubed ham. Heat through.

Place two eggs on each plate, pour the curry sauce over and decorate with lemon slices and chopped parsley.

1 Bring half-filled saucepan of water to boil. Add 1 × 5ml tsp (1tsp) salt. Slide egg from saucer into water.

2 Gather white around yolk using large spoon. Simmer (not boil) for approx 3–4min.

3 Lift out eggs with slotted spoon and put into cold or hot water depending on how you intend to serve them.

Fried and Baked Eggs

It is possible to make the most delicate and intricate dishes with eggs, but eggs are also something to turn to when times are hard and something good and filling is needed for lunch or supper.

Fried Eggs

This is a more unusual method of frying eggs – usually done in hotter lard or oil until the whites are brown and crispy on the outside. Here, butter is used (which gives a rich taste to the eggs), and the eggs are gently cooked by basting them with the butter, rather than fried. See the illustrations and captions on the right for detailed instructions.

Always keep the heat low and baste every few minutes with the melted butter in the pan.

If you haven't got any sort of metal ring, you can of course cut the white of the egg, once cooked, to get the desired effect.

Eggs can be fried with the yolks whole 'sunny side up', or the yolks can be broken so that they spread out in the pan, or they can be fried on both sides, 'over easy' as the Americans say.

Different fats give different flavours, but butter is by far the best to use.

Nest Eggs

Allow 1 or 2 eggs and 2 anchovy fillets per person

Separate the yolks and the whites. Keep the yolks in their half-shells. In a large clean bowl, beat the whites until stiff and then put them into well-buttered oven-proof individual ramekins. Make a hollow in each egg-white, and lay a yolk carefully in it. Cross anchovy fillets on top of the yolks. Bake the eggs in their nests in a warm oven until the yolks are fairly firm. Serve with hot, buttered toast.

Baked Egg Surprise

(serves 4)

12 slices mild skinless salami or thick smoked sausage
8 eggs
8 slices cheese (Gruyère or Emmenthal)

Melt a little butter in a large frying pan and put in the slices of sausage. Break the eggs on top, and place a slice of cheese on each egg. Put a lid on the pan and fry over low heat until the eggs are firm and the cheese has melted.

Fried Eggs

1 Melt some butter over a low heat in the frying pan. Break one egg at a time into a saucer and let it slip gently down into the frying pan.

2 The eggs should be basted, not fried. Baste the eggs with the melted butter now and then which will give them a shiny, smooth surface.

Deep-fried Eggs

Eggs can also be deep-fried in lard or oil, in a chip pan.

Heat the oil until smoking hot. The eggs *must* be fresh, otherwise they will make the fat spit and possibly bubble over. Pour each egg into a saucer and slip it carefully into the fat. It should cook until the white is firm (about 2–3 min). Lift out with a slotted spoon, and let it drain well on some paper towels. Sprinkle with a little salt, and serve with bacon and fresh bread.

A substantial midday snack. Brown sliced carrots, onions and leek rings in hot butter, add baked beans and seasoning, and top with fried or poached eggs.

Luxury Eggs

Allow 1 egg, 2 slices of smoked salmon and a little finely chopped chives per person

Cut the slices of salmon into strips and put them into small, buttered, oven-proof ramekins. Sprinkle with the chopped chives, and then slip the eggs gently on top (the yolks must be whole). Season with freshly ground pepper, and some salt if you like (the salmon will be salty). Bake the eggs in a warm oven until the whites have set. Serve with fresh white bread and a green salad.

3 If you want to have very special fried eggs which are circular and identical in size, you can buy special egg rings (or you can use the metal rings from preserving jars).

Baked Egg Custard and Scrambled Eggs

Both cost so little and taste so good! A few eggs, a little cream, milk or water, is all that is needed to make a delicious snack, a breakfast, or a light lunch or supper. Serve by themselves with bread, or more substantially, accompanying meat, smoked fish or vegetables.

Baked Egg Custard
Baked egg custard is made from beaten eggs, milk, or milk and cream mixed, and seasoning.
The mixture is put into well-buttered ramekins, a circular or oblong baking dish, and is baked in a hot water bath at a low temperature until firm. The finished custard should be smooth and without holes.

Baked Egg Custard
(serves 4)
Baking time: 35–40 min
Oven temperature: 160°C, 325°F, Gas 3

200ml (7fl oz) milk
4 eggs
$\frac{1}{2} \times 5ml$ tsp ($\frac{1}{2}$tsp) salt

1 Let the milk come to the boil and then cool. Beat the eggs carefully

Scrambled Eggs with Crab is both simple and tasty, and a good way of using canned crab.

Baked Egg Custard

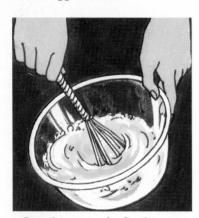

1 Beat the eggs gently. Set the oven at the required temperature.

2 Add the cooled boiled milk and salt, and stir it all carefully together.

3 Butter a baking dish very thoroughly (or individual ramekins), and pour the mixture into the dish.

together, but not too hard, as the air bubbles will make the texture too porous.

Add milk and salt and stir together.
2 Pour the mixture into a well-buttered baking dish (or individual ramekins). Put the baking dish (or ramekins) into an oven tray filled with water to reach half-way up the dish. Bake the custard (ramekins will require only about 10–20 min) and cut it into slices or cubes and serve with smoked fish, smoked ham or with a creamed vegetable, like spinach.

Scrambled Eggs with Crab
(serves 4)

6–8 eggs
12–16 × 15ml tbsp (12–16tbsp)
  double cream
salt and pepper to taste
butter
1 small tin crab meat
fresh dill

1 Beat together eggs, cream, salt and pepper. Divide the crab meat into pieces and chop the dill finely.
2 Melt a little butter in a thick-bottomed saucepan. Pour in the egg mixture and let it thicken over low heat. Stir now and then with a wooden spoon. When the scrambled eggs are ready they should have thickened, but the mixture should be moist and creamy – not dry. Put it in a serving dish and sprinkle generously with the finely chopped dill. Put the pieces of crab on top. Serve this dish piping hot, with French bread or toast, butter and a good salad.

4 Put the dish into an oven tray filled with water to come halfway up the sides. Bake for the required time.

Ham Rolls filled with Scrambled Eggs on Spinach.

Ham Rolls filled with Scrambled Eggs on Spinach
(serves 4)

6 slices cooked ham
4 eggs
8 × 15ml tbsp (8tbsp) water or double cream
salt and white pepper to taste
175g (6oz) grated cheese (Gruyère or Emmenthal)
675g (1½lb) spinach or equivalent weight of frozen, chopped spinach
nutmeg

1 Beat together eggs, water or cream, and salt and pepper.
Melt a little butter in a thick-bottomed saucepan. Pour in the egg mixture and stir carefully with a wooden spoon over low heat. When

the scrambled eggs are thick and creamy, they are ready. Take off heat immediately, and cool.
2 Thaw the frozen spinach and press out the water. Fresh spinach should be chopped. Steam the spinach in a little butter and season with salt, pepper and nutmeg. Grease a medium baking dish with butter and spread the spinach in it.
3 Put the cold scrambled eggs on the slices of ham and roll them up as illustrated. Put the ham rolls on top of the spinach and sprinkle the grated cheese on top. Heat in the oven (200°C, 400°F, Gas 6) until the cheese browns. This dish can be prepared in advance and heated through just before serving.
Serve with bread and butter.

Omelettes

When one considers how modest basic omelettes are – both in terms of ingredients and the cooking method – it is surprising how few cooks agree on how to cook and prepare them. But however made – as you like it, for preference – omelettes are tasty, filling, easy and of infinite variety.

Omelette Tips

● Beat the eggs lightly just before you are about to make the omelette.
● Use a very clean frying pan, preferably one with rounded edges.
● Don't make your omelettes too large.
● Pour the egg mixture into the pan when the butter has melted and has stopped sizzling.
● Let the mixture begin to set over a moderate heat before you begin to lift it.
● Push the mixture towards the centre around the pan, so that the liquid egg sets along the edges.
● Take the pan off the burner just before the consistency is right.
● Loosen the omelette round the edges with a knife or a spatula.
● Fold the omelette in two or three and leave in the pan for a while before you slip it onto a warm plate.
● Brush the surface with a little melted butter.

Basic Omelette

Filled omelettes can be made in two ways; you can either combine the filling with the liquid egg mixture, or place it on half the cooked omelette before it is folded. Sweet dessert omelettes always have the filling added after the omelette is cooked. Although many cooks claim that omelettes are difficult to cook successfully, don't be put off. Even if they break up, they'll still taste delicious as long as the basic rules have been followed – fresh eggs, good butter, and a moderate heat.

Special omelette pans are available, but they must be treated very carefully. They must never be used for anything else.

They should never be washed, just rubbed clean with paper and possibly a little coarse salt while still warm. Wrap in paper and put aside until needed again.

Basic Omelette
(per person)

2 eggs
2 × 15ml tbsp (2tbsp) single cream or water
salt and white pepper to taste

Beat eggs, cream and seasoning lightly and cook the omelette as explained under *Omelette Tips*, and in the illustrations below.

VARIATIONS

Mushroom
Chop fresh mushrooms and sauté them lightly in butter. Mix carefully into the egg mixture.

Herb
Chop fresh, green herbs (such as parsley, chives, tarragon or chervil) finely, and mix them into the egg mixture. About $\frac{1}{2}$ × 15ml tbsp ($\frac{1}{2}$tbsp) herbs per person.

Cheese
Mix grated cheese into the egg mixture.

Onion
Chop onion coarsely and sauté it in a little butter until light golden in colour. Mix it into the egg mixture.

Omelette Gratinée
Make a basic omelette, and fill it if you like. Place the finished omelette on a buttered baking dish and sprinkle 3–4 × 15ml tbsp (3–4tbsp) grated cheese on top (Cheddar is best). Dot with butter. Put the baking dish into a preheated oven (220°C, 425°F, Gas 7) for about 10–15 min, or until the omelette is golden brown and the cheese has melted. Or you can brown it under a hot grill.

Soufflé Omelette
(per person)

1 egg
salt
1 × 15ml tbsp (1tbsp) double cream
6g ($\frac{1}{4}$oz) butter

1 Separate the egg, and beat the yolk with a little salt. Beat the white and the cream separately until stiff. Mix everything together when the butter in the pan is warm.

1 Beat the eggs and salt lightly together with a whisk or a fork. Do not beat for too long.

2 Melt plenty of butter in the pan and pour the egg mixture in when it is melted and hot, but not brown.

3 Keep the egg mixture moving. Shake the pan and loosen the omelette from the sides with a spatula.

An appetizing first course or supper dish : omelette filled with warm asparagus tips, garnished with finely chopped parsley.

2 Pour the mixture into the pan and leave the omelette until set over a moderate heat.

This omelette will be high and fluffy. Serve it on its own or with creamed vegetables, bacon, mushrooms or cheese.

VARIATION
Substitute sugar for the salt, and serve the omelette as a dessert, with fruit, jam, or fresh berries.

Basic Dessert Omelette
(per person)

2 eggs
2 × 15ml tbsp (2tbsp) single cream or
*   water*
a little sugar

Beat the eggs together lightly with the cream and cook the omelette as described in the Basic Omelette recipe and the pictures. Always fill dessert omelettes after cooking.

Basic Omelette (below) is folded over carefully and transferred to a warm platter.

4 Fold the omelette carefully in two or three. Let it lie in the pan for a while and then slip it onto a warm platter.

Stuffed Omelettes

Omelette with Spinach Cream
(serves 4)

Make an omelette following the basic recipe and fill it with spinach cream.

40g (1½oz) butter
3 × 15ml tbsp (3tbsp) flour
300–400ml (½–¾pt) milk or single cream
salt, white pepper
nutmeg
1 large packet frozen spinach

Melt the butter and add the flour. Add milk or cream, stirring all the while, and leave the sauce to simmer for approximately 5 min. Mix in the thawed spinach and season to taste. Put the creamed spinach on half the omelette and fold the other half over.

Liver, Onion and Mushroom Omelette
(serves 4)

6 eggs
10–12 × 15ml tbsp (10–12tbsp) double cream or water
1 × 5ml tsp (1tsp) salt
½ × 5ml tsp (½tsp) white pepper
butter for frying
For the filling:
10–12 shallots or button onions
250g (9oz) mushrooms, chopped
250g (9oz) frozen chicken livers
about 100g (4oz) butter
200ml (7fl oz) bouillon or stock
½ × 15ml tbsp (½tbsp) flour
salt and pepper
dry sherry (optional)

1 Wash and peel the onions. Brown them lightly in butter and put aside. Now, and between each browning process, add a little stock to the frying pan to deglaze, seasoning with salt, pepper and the sherry (if used). Keep the liquid.

Brown the chopped mushrooms in butter quickly over a fairly high heat and mix them with the onions.

2 Thaw chicken livers, dry and coat in flour, and brown in butter for 4–5 min. Mix the livers with the onions and mushrooms. Add the seasoned stock-liquid to the vegetable and liver mixture, and keep warm.

3 Heat a little butter in a clean frying or omelette pan. Beat the eggs, cream and seasonings lightly together, and pour into the pan. Cook the basic omelette (see page 16), and fold it around the filling.

Shrimp Omelette
(serves 4)

225g (½lb) cleaned shrimps
2 × 15ml tbsp (2tbsp) finely chopped dill

Make an omelette following the basic recipe, and top with the shrimps and dill while still a little creamy.

Kipper Omelette
(serves 4)

2 kippers, boned
4 eggs
3 × 15ml tbsp (3tbsp) milk
salt and pepper
25g (1oz) butter
finely chopped parsley

Make the omelette according to the basic recipe. Just before it's ready, put thin strips of the boned fish on

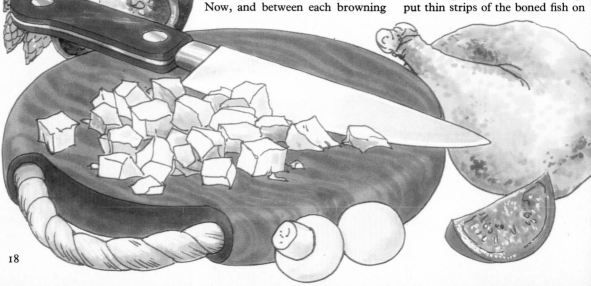

An omelette is what you make it. The filling here is a delicious, creamed mixture of chicken livers, mushrooms and onions.

top. Fold the omelette in two, sprinkle a little parsley on top and serve it with thick slices of buttered toast.

Tomato Omelette
Make an omelette following the basic recipe, and place slices of tomato on top while still creamy. Sprinkle with finely chopped chives.

Smoked Salmon Omelette
Make a basic omelette, and top with thin slices of smoked salmon and a sprinkling of chopped chives when the omelette is nearly ready. Serve with generously buttered, thin brown-bread toast.

King-size Omelette
Make one basic omelette, and top with slices of tomato. Do *not* fold it. Put it into an ovenproof dish and keep it warm in the oven. Make a second basic omelette, and fill with lightly cooked vegetables (frozen vegetables are suitable). Put one of the omelettes on top of the other, and sprinkle generously with grated

cheese. Grill or bake for a few minutes until the cheese melts.

Dessert Omelettes
Make the omelette following the basic recipe on page 17. Fill it with sweetened whole soft fruit or with a soft fruit purée, or with tinned fruit cut in thin slices. Sprinkle with icing sugar or chopped nuts. Make a chequered pattern in the icing sugar by pressing a hot skewer criss-cross on it.

A sweet omelette can also be filled with slices of vanilla icecream or butterscotch icecream, with a topping of caramel or chocolate sauce, or a soft fruit purée.

Brown the sausages lightly while the omelette is cooking. Lift the egg mixture now and then with a spatula from the sides and in the middle so that the liquid runs down into the pan.

colour in a little butter, lay them on the omelette and sprinkle finely chopped herbs on top. Serve the omelette immediately, with bread, butter and mustard.

Basque Omelette
(serves 4)

1 green pepper
4 tomatoes
1 can tuna fish in oil
4–6 eggs
1 × 15ml tbsp (1 tbsp) double cream
¼ × 5ml tsp (¼ tsp) salt
white pepper
4 anchovy fillets
1 × 15ml tbsp (1 tbsp) finely chopped parsley

1 Cut the pepper in thin strips. Dip the tomatoes for a moment in boiling water, skin and cut them into wedges. Drain the tuna fish of oil (which you keep), and divide the fish into chunks.
2 Heat the oil from the tuna in a frying pan and fry the strips of pepper gently for a few minutes. Add the tomato wedges and the pieces of tuna, and let them simmer a few more minutes.
3 Beat the eggs with cream, salt and a little pepper, and pour the mixture into the frying pan. Put the anchovy fillets on top, and let the omelette cook and set over low heat. Sprinkle chopped parsley over the omelette and serve with fresh white bread and butter.

More Substantial Omelettes

Sausage Omelette
(serves 4)

4–6 eggs
½ × 5ml tsp (½ tsp) salt
pepper
2 × 5ml tsp (2 tsp) flour
100ml (4fl oz) milk
25g (1oz) butter

Filling and garnish :
1 small can cocktail sausages
1 × 15ml tbsp (1 tbsp) finely chopped parsley or chives

1 Mix the eggs, flour, salt and pepper and beat together. Beat in the milk gradually.
2 Melt the butter in the frying pan and pour in the egg mixture. Allow the omelette to thicken over low heat. Lift up the edges gently now and then with a spatula, so that the liquid egg runs down into the pan.
3 Sauté the sausages to a golden

A Basque Omelette makes a colourful and filling lunch or supper. The anchovy fillets add an extra piquancy.

Basque Omelette

1 Sauté the pepper strips in oil for a few minutes. Add the skinned tomato wedges and the tuna and sauté for a few more minutes.

2 Beat together eggs, cream, salt and pepper and pour the mixture into the pan.

Country Omelette
(serves 4)

1 onion
1 green pepper
4 medium, boiled potatoes, peeled
225g (½lb) smoked pork sausage
butter
salt and pepper
½ × 5ml tsp (½tsp) finely chopped
*   marjoram*
finely chopped parsley and chives
Basic Omelette mixture (see page 16)

1 Chop the onion and cut the pepper into strips. Skin the pork sausage and cut into slices. Cut the cooked potato into cubes.
2 Sauté onion, pepper, sausage slices and cubed potatoes in butter in the frying pan. Season with salt, pepper and marjoram.
3 Pour the egg mixture over and let it set over a low heat. Lift the sides of the omelette now and then with a spatula, so that the liquid egg mixture runs down onto the bottom of the pan. When ready, the omelette should be firm, but still soft and moist on top. Sprinkle chopped parsley and chives on top, and serve the omelette straight from the pan.

Smoked Fish Omelette
(serves 4)

1 smoked mackerel (or other smoked
*   fish)*
4 tomatoes
salt and pepper
25g (1oz) butter
1 × 15ml tbsp (1tbsp) chopped chives
Basic Omelette mixture (see page 16)

1 Remove the skin and bones from the fish and divide it into bite-sized pieces. Cut the tomatoes into wedges and season lightly.
2 Melt a little butter in the frying pan. Put in the pieces of fish and the tomato wedges.
3 Pour the omelette mixture over the filling and let the omelette set over low heat. Use a spatula and lift the omelette now and then, so that the mixture runs down into the pan. Sprinkle with finely chopped chives.

One basic omelette mixture, but with deliciously different fillings. Left, with smoked fish. Right above, a Country Omelette. Right below, with bacon, and with curried shrimps.

Curried Shrimp Omelette

(serves 4)

25g (1oz) butter
1 × 5ml tsp (1tsp) curry powder
1 small onion
1 green pepper
100g (4oz) peeled shrimps
Basic Omelette mixture (see page 16)

1 Sauté the curry powder for a few seconds in the butter. Chop the onion and the pepper finely, and sauté them in the curry butter until soft and golden. Add the shrimps and let them heat through for a moment (they must not actually *cook*, as this makes them tough).
2 Pour the egg mixture over the filling and let the omelette set, but not go dry, over low heat. Lift with a spatula now and then so that the liquid egg runs down into the pan. Serve the omelette piping hot with fresh bread and a salad.

Bacon Omelette

(serves 4)

8 bacon rashers
1 sprig parsley
Basic Omelette mixture (see page 16)

1 Fry the bacon until brown and crisp in its own fat.
2 Pour the omelette mixture over the bacon and fry the omelette over low heat until it is firm but still creamy. Sprinkle finely chopped parsley on top and serve with bread.

Soufflé dishes
1 Use a soufflé dish with high, straight sides. Cut out a higher collar of greaseproof paper.

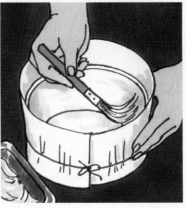

2 Fasten the collar with string or a couple of paper clips. Dip a pastry brush in melted butter and grease the dish and collar thoroughly.

3 As soon as the egg whites and the sauce are folded together, pour the soufflé mixture into the dish. It must not be more than ¼ full.

Soufflés – Light and Delicious

No dish generates as much enthusiasm and appreciation as a high, light soufflé. Soufflés can be savoury or sweet, and although generally thought difficult, are really quite simple to make – as long as certain rules are strictly adhered to. See the individual recipes for further hints, but two of these rules are very basic: never open the oven door while the soufflé is baking, and it must *be served directly from the oven.*

Basic Soufflé
(serves 4)

Preparation time: about 15 min
Baking time: about 40 min
Oven temperature: 180°C, 350°F, Gas 4

*4 eggs, separated
25g (1oz) butter
4 × 15ml tbsp (4tbsp) flour
150ml (¼pt) milk
150ml (¼pt) single cream*

Melt the butter, stir in the flour and gradually add the milk and cream. Stir constantly until the sauce is smooth. Let it cook for a few minutes, remove the saucepan from the heat and leave the sauce to cool.
2 Beat the egg yolks together, and stir them gradually into the sauce.
3 Beat the egg whites until stiff. Stir

about ¼ whipped egg whites into the sauce, and then fold this mixture lightly into the remaining whites.
4 Butter a soufflé baking dish with high, straight sides, put a collar of greaseproof paper around the edge (see above) and pour the soufflé mixture into the baking dish. Bake in the centre of a preheated oven (180°C, 350°F, Gas 4) oven for about 40 min.
Serve the soufflé straight from the oven, otherwise it will fall. Soufflés are very sensitive to draughts or jolts, and must be handled carefully.

Simple Savoury Soufflé
Make the soufflé following the basic recipe above, but season the sauce with salt and pepper.
Serve the soufflé with creamed seafood, mushrooms or vegetables, and fresh, crisp French bread.

Basic Soufflé
1 Melt butter in a saucepan. Add flour and stir well.

2 Add the milk or cream and stir until smooth. Leave to simmer for a few minutes.

3 Remove the sauce from the heat, cool slightly, and stir in the beaten egg yolks, a little at a time.

4 Take the soufflé out of the oven. Remove the collar and serve immediately.

Vanilla Soufflé

Make the soufflé according to the basic recipe, but add 2 × 15ml tbsp (2tbsp) sugar and 1½ × 15ml tbsp (1½tbsp) vanilla sugar to the sauce. (Make vanilla sugar by storing two vanilla pods in a canister of sugar. Shake occasionally.)
Serve this soufflé with soft or tinned fruit.

Orange Soufflé

Follow the basic recipe, but add 2 × 15ml tbsp (2tbsp) sugar and the grated peel and juice of 1 orange.

Lemon Soufflé

Follow the basic recipe, but add 3 × 15ml tbsp (3tbsp) sugar, the grated peel of 1 lemon and the juice of ½ lemon.

4 Add any seasonings or flavourings, such as cheese, fruit, melted chocolate, etc.

5 Beat the egg whites until so stiff that the bowl can be turned upside down. (An added pinch of salt helps.)

6 Stir in ¼ of whites into sauce, pour into remaining whites, fold together carefully.

Vegetable Soufflé (left)
(serves 4)

½kg (about 2lb) cooked, sliced
    vegetables (cauliflower, peas,
    leeks, beans)
For the sauce :
20g (¾oz) butter
3 × 15ml tbsp (3tbsp) flour
300ml (½pt) milk or single cream
4 eggs, separated
salt and white pepper

1 Melt the butter, stir in the flour,
and add the milk a little at a time.
Add the beaten egg yolks.
2 Let the sauce simmer for a few
minutes and then add the cooked,
sliced vegetables. Season with salt
and pepper and add the stiffly beaten
egg whites (see pages 24–25).
2 Pour the mixture into the soufflé
dish and bake in a preheated oven
(180°C, 350°F, Gas 4) for about
45 min.
Serve with white bread or individual
rolls, and a green salad.

Cheese Soufflé
(serves 4)

3 × 15ml tbsp (3tbsp) flour
25g (1oz) butter
300ml (½pt) milk
½ × 5ml tsp (½tsp) salt
    3 eggs, separated
200g (7oz) Cheddar cheese, cubed
25g (1oz) grated Cheddar cheese

1 Make a thick sauce with the
butter, flour and milk. Leave to cool.
2 Stir in the egg yolks, the salt and
cheese cubes. Beat the egg whites
stiff and fold them carefully into the
cheese mixture.
3 Butter a baking dish and pour in
the thick cheese mixture. Sprinkle a
little grated cheese on top and bake
the soufflé for about 50 min in a
preheated oven (200°C, 400°F, Gas
6).
Serve the cheese soufflé as a supper
dish with bread or rolls and butter.

VARIATION
Add to the cheese sauce about 100g
(4oz) chopped celeriac (blanched in
boiling water for about 10 min) and
50–100g (2–4oz) fried, chopped
bacon. The sauce could be made
with the stock from the celeriac
blanching and a little cream instead
of milk.

Clam Soufflé (right)
(serves 5–6)

1 can clams (about 250g or 9oz)
25g (1oz) butter
3½ × 15ml tbsp (3½tbsp) flour
400ml (¾pt) milk
4 eggs, separated
2 × 15ml tbsp (2tbsp) finely chopped
dill, parsley or tarragon
salt, white pepper

1 Strain off the liquid from the clams and chop them coarsely.
2 Melt the butter, stir in the flour and add the milk a little at a time. Let the sauce simmer for a few minutes, then remove from the heat. Let it cool a little and stir in the egg yolks, one at a time. Add finely chopped herbs, salt and pepper and the coarsely chopped clams.
3 Beat the egg whites stiff and fold them carefully into the soufflé mixture.
4 Pour the mixture into a buttered and floured baking dish, and bake for about 45 min in a preheated oven (180°C, 350°F, Gas 4) until high and golden.
Serve with salad, white bread, and parsley butter (mix finely chopped parsley into soft butter and then cool).

Asparagus Soufflé (right)
(serves 4)

1 can asparagus
1 small packet frozen peas
For the sauce:
20–25g (¾–1oz) butter
3 × 15ml tbsp (3tbsp) flour
300ml (½pt) milk or single cream
4 eggs, separated
salt and white pepper

1 Strain off the liquid from the asparagus and cut them into chunks. Parboil the peas.
2 Melt the butter, stir in the flour and add milk or cream. Let the sauce cook a few minutes. Cool a little and stir in the egg yolks one at a time. Add the vegetables and seasoning.
3 Beat the egg whites stiff and fold them carefully into the sauce. Then pour everything into a buttered and floured baking dish and bake for about 45 min in a preheated oven (180°C, 350°F, Gas 4).
Serve with parsley butter (see previous recipe) and white bread.

Chocolate Soufflé (left)

(serves 4)
Preparation time: about 20 min
Baking time: 30–40 min
Oven temperature: 180°C, 350°F,
Gas 4

3 × 15ml tbsp (3tbsp) butter
3 × 15ml tbsp (3tbsp) flour
about 250ml (9fl oz) milk
4 eggs, separated, plus 1 white
about 50g (2oz) sugar
75g (3oz) cooking chocolate,
icing sugar

1 Melt the butter, stir in the flour
and add the milk gradually. Let the
sauce simmer for a couple of
minutes and leave to cool.
2 Melt the chocolate in a bowl in
warm water and stir it into the sauce.
3 Beat the egg yolks and sugar
together until thick and stir into the
sauce. Beat the 5 egg whites until
stiff and fold them carefully into the
sauce mixture. Pour into a well-
buttered and sugared baking dish
and bake for 30–40 min in a preheated oven (180°C, 350°F, Gas 4).

Fruit Soufflé (right)
(serves 4)
Preparation time: about 15 min
Baking time: 30–40 min
Oven temperature: 180–200°C,
350–400°F, Gas 4–6

6–8 peaches, apricots, apples, pears
  or equivalent, fresh or canned
40g (1½oz) butter
3 × 15ml tbsp (3tbsp) flour
250ml (9fl oz) milk
3–4 eggs, separated
1 × 15ml tbsp (1tbsp) sugar
grated rind of ½ lemon

1 Peel, slice the fruit in half and
cook until tender in a light syrup
(sugar and water). Drain well. Drain
canned fruit.
2 Place the fruit in a buttered dish.
3 Melt the butter, stir in the flour
and add milk. Simmer sauce gently
for a few minutes, leave to cool.
4 Stir in the egg yolks and add sugar
and grated lemon rind.
5 Beat the egg whites stiff, and fold
into the sauce. Pour the mixture
over the fruit and bake for
30–40 min in the preheated oven.

Grandma's Apple Soufflé (left)
(serves 4)
Preparation time: about 30 min
Baking time: 40–45 min
Oven temperature: 180°C, 350°F,
Gas 4

½kg (1¼lb) apples
2 × 15ml tbsp (2tbsp) sugar
lemon juice
1 cup water
5 eggs, separated
175g (6oz) sugar
250g (9oz) ground almonds
50g(2oz) flour
250ml (9fl oz) double cream

1 Peel and slice the apples. Cook
until tender in the water, with 2tbsp
sugar and lemon juice. Drain and
put in a buttered dish.
2 Beat the egg yolks and half the
sugar until stiff and creamy. Mix the
ground almonds with the flour and
sift into the egg mixture.
3 Beat the egg whites until very stiff
and then add the remaining sugar
gradually, beating continuously.
Then fold the egg white into the
egg-yolk mixture.
4 Pour the batter over the apples
and bake on the lowest oven rack.

Say Cheese . . .

Cheese doesn't always have to play the main part in a dish. Added in small amounts, cheese gives both flavour and richness to cold and hot dishes. Cheese goes well with almost anything. It can be sprinkled over a dish to be grilled or baked; it can be melted in sauces, or on bread for a snack; and it can serve as a filling for both meat and fish.

A good example is onion soup with cheese-topped slices of French bread – a filling and delicious soup, associated with the famous Les Halles Market in Paris (which, alas, no longer exists). Cheese and meat are often served together in many national cuisines, and thin slices of veal or pork sandwiching cheese and smoked ham are delicious. Another variation – from Italy – is a tasty pork or veal cutlet. Cut a pocket in the cutlet and put in a slice of cheese.

Turn the cutlet first in beaten egg and then in fine breadcrumbs mixed with salt, pepper and finely chopped basil. Fry in butter until golden.

Macaroni Cheese
Make a white sauce of butter, flour and milk and let it cook for a few minutes. Stir in about 175g (6oz) grated cheese (Gruyère, Emmenthal or Cheddar), and season with salt, pepper and grated nutmeg. Add cooked macaroni and

serve sprinkled with finely chopped parsley. This is delicious with fried sausages or bacon, and is a good, filling everyday meal.

Frankfurters with Cheese Filling
Allow 2–3 grilling Frankfurter sausages per person. Make a deep cut lengthwise in the Frankfurters and put a thin stick of cheese in the cut. Use Cheddar, Gruyère or Emmenthal. Wrap a slice of bacon around each Frankfurter to hold the cheese in place, and fasten with a wooden cocktail stick. Put the Frankfurters in an ovenproof dish or pan and bake in a hot oven (200°C, 400°F, Gas 6) until the cheese is melted and the bacon slices are brown and crisp. Serve with mashed potatoes with lots of chopped chives, or baked potatoes with sour cream and chives.

Fish with Spinach and Cheese
Thaw a packet of frozen, chopped spinach. Squeeze out most of the water and put the spinach in a buttered, ovenproof dish. Sprinkle on a little onion salt. Place a thawed block of fish (cod is best) on top of the spinach and then sprinkle with about 250g (9oz) grated cheese and a little nutmeg. Pour about 200ml (7fl oz) cream into the baking dish and put in a hot oven (200°C, 400°F, Gas 6) for 30–40 min. Serve with boiled potatoes or rice.

Scalloped Potatoes with Cheese
Peel 8–10 medium potatoes and slice thinly. Grate about 200g (7oz) cheese (Cheddar, Gruyère or Emmenthal), and cut 2 medium leeks into thin rings. Put the potatoes, leeks and cheese in layers in a buttered baking dish and sprinkle a little salt and pepper between each layer. Pour 200–300ml (7–10fl oz) cream into the baking dish and bake in a moderately hot oven (180°C, 350°F, Gas 4) for about 1 hr. This dish is very filling, and is a delicious accompaniment to any kind of fried food or cold meats.

Cheese Salads
Fresh salad greens, fruit and pieces of cheese go well together. For example, mix crisp lettuce leaves (iceberg or Cos), chopped celery, diced apple and cubes of cheese (you could use a Swiss or Dutch cheese, Jarlsberg, Cheddar – or, more adventurously, Mozzarella). Dress this salad with a French dressing, or one made of sour cream and mayonnaise, lemon juice, salt, pepper and finely chopped walnuts.
Or you can let cheese flavour a dressing, to serve with a simple green salad. Mash a little piece of any blue cheese with a fork. Mix 3 × 15ml tbsp (3tbsp) olive oil, 2 × 15ml tbsp (2tbsp) vinegar, salt, pepper and a little garlic salt in a small jar. Put the lid on tightly, and shake until everything is well mixed. Add the cheese and shake vigorously again. Make this dressing in quite large amounts. It keeps well in the refrigerator.

Grated Cheese
A simple bouillon, clear soup or vegetable soup becomes much more interesting with a sprinkle of cheese on top. Put a dish of finely grated Parmesan on the table, and let everyone help themselves. Lots of dishes are enhanced by grated hard cheese, but pasta without Parmesan is unthinkable!

Cheese Bread
Butter slices of white bread and sprinkle plenty of grated cheese on top (Swiss cheese is the best). Lay the bread slices on a baking tray and bake in a hot oven until the cheese is melted and golden in colour. This is the traditional accompaniment for French onion soup.
Garlic bread with cheese is an exciting alternative to plain French bread or rolls on special occasions.
Halve a French loaf lengthwise, and lay the two pieces on a baking tray with the cut side uppermost. Melt 100g (4oz) butter and pour it over the cut surfaces. Mix 150–175g (5–6oz) grated Parmesan with 2 × 15ml tbsp (2tbsp) finely chopped parsley. 1 × 5ml tsp (1tsp) paprika, and garlic powder to taste. Sprinkle the mixture over the cut surfaces and put the loaves into a hot oven, (200°C, 400°F, Gas 6) until the loaves are hot and the surface is golden in colour. Cut into chunky slices and serve them hot.
This garlic bread may be served with all kinds of dishes and goes especially well with casseroles.

add this, stirring continuously. Serve as Swiss Cheese Fondue with cubed French bread, accompanied by beer or white wine.

Deep-fried Camembert (left)

Small, deep-fried wedges of Camembert served with blackcurrant jam or grapes makes a delicious and different dessert (or starter).

As it only takes a few moments to cook, allow your guests to have a little rest after the main course while you heat the deep fat for frying.

You need 3 wedges of Camembert per person, 1 egg, fine breadcrumbs, and lard or oil for the deep-frying. The cheese must be ripe, but should be chilled. Coat the cheese first with beaten egg and then with fine breadcrumbs. (This can be done well in advance, and left in the refrigerator, so that it is ready for deep-frying.) Heat the oil or lard until smoking hot. Deep-fry the cheese wedges for a few seconds only, until they are golden and crisp on the outside (but still soft inside). Drain the cheese on a paper towel and serve hot with grapes and chopped walnuts or blackcurrant jam. A gooseberry sauce is a good accompaniment.

Swiss Cheese Fondue
(serves 4)

1 clove garlic
1 × 15ml tbsp (1tbsp) lemon juice
350ml (12fl oz) dry white wine
700g (1½lb) Gruyère or Emmenthal, grated
2 heaped × 5ml tsp (2tsp) cornflour
2 × 15ml tbsp (2tbsp) cognac
white pepper
grated nutmeg
paprika

1 Rub the inside of an earthenware fireproof dish, a fondue dish, or a heavy-bottomed saucepan with the clove of garlic.
2 Add the white wine and lemon juice and warm over a very low heat. Add the grated cheese gradually, stirring all the time.
3 When the cheese has completely melted and the mixture is smooth, add the cornflour which has been blended with the cognac. Stir well until the mixture begins to bubble, and let it simmer for about 3 min. Season to taste with pepper and nutmeg.

4 Cut a day-old French loaf into cubes. Place the pan or fondue dish on a table-top burner and let everyone help themselves. The bread cubes are stuck onto a fondue fork, dipped into the cheese until coated, and then eaten while piping hot. A dry white wine is good with this dish.

English Cheese Fondue
(serves 2–3)

250ml (9fl oz) beer
250g (9oz) grated Cheddar cheese
1 clove garlic
25g (1oz) butter
2 × 15ml tbsp (2tbsp) cornflour
½ × 5ml tsp (½tsp) dry mustard
3 × 15ml tbsp (3tbsp) beer

A special fondue dish is best, but a heavy saucepan can be used instead (it just doesn't look so good).
1 Put the larger quantity of beer, cheese and crushed clove of garlic into the fondue dish and stir slowly until the cheese has melted. Stir in the butter.
2 Blend the cornflour and the dry mustard into the remaining beer and

American Cheese Fondue
(serves 2–3)

1 clove garlic
200g (7oz) grated Cheddar cheese
100g (4oz) grated Swiss cheese
125ml (4½fl oz) concentrated tomato juice (or canned tomato soup)
1 × 5ml tsp (1tsp) Worcestershire sauce
3 × 15ml tbsp (3tbsp) dry sherry
Frankfurter sausages
French bread

1 Rub the inside of your chosen fondue dish with the clove of garlic. Add the cheese, tomato juice or soup and Worcestershire sauce. Stir well over low heat until the cheese has completely melted (the mixture should have a creamy consistency). Stir in the sherry and leave to simmer for 2–3 min.
2 Cut the Frankfurters into small pieces and the bread into cubes. Stick the pieces of Frankfurter sausage and bread onto the fondue fork and dip into the cheese mixture. Red wine or beer may be served with this dish.

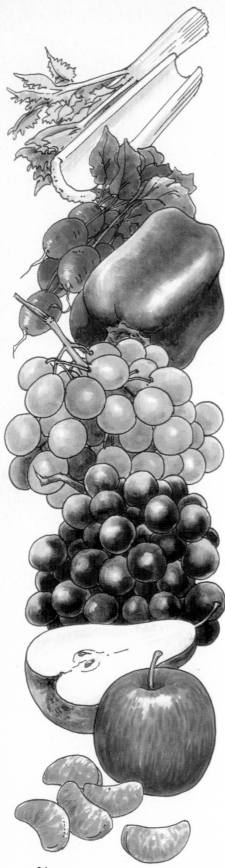

A Party Cheese Board

Assemble a few well-chosen cheeses, a selection of biscuits or French loaves, a little fruit and something good to drink – and you have the makings of a party.

On the introductory pages there is a listing of many different types of cheese. Here we suggest which types of cheese go together, and how much cheese should be allowed per person. A cheese board is suitable for all occasions and can be prepared very simply. If you are only serving cheese and nothing else, you should allow about 200g (7oz) cheese per person, and serve a wide variety, including soft cheeses, like Brie or Camembert, harder cheeses like Gruyère or Leicester, and the sharper blue cheeses. Arrange them on a board or serving dish and decorate with fruit and vegetables.

For a cheese board for 12, we would suggest the following amounts.

700g (1½lb) good farmhouse
 Cheddar
400g (14oz) Leicester
400g (14oz) Port Salut
400g (14oz) blue cheese (both
 Stilton and Dolcelatte, for
 instance)
300g (11oz) Brie or Camembert
200g (7oz) of more unusual cheeses,
 like Boursin, a Chèvre or a
 Geitost
1 head of celery
450g (1lb) white grapes
450g (1lb) black grapes
1 pear
1 red apple
1 red pepper
1 sprig parsley

Serve the cheese with French bread, or a variety of biscuits, and butter. Almost any drink is suitable: tea, mineral water, soft drinks, beer, apple juice, or wine.

Always put enough cheese knives on the serving table. There should be at least one for the mild cheeses and one for the sharp ones. Have a cheese slicer available for something like a Norwegian geitost.

Cheese for Dessert

If cheese is to be the finale to a meal, serve it with a little fruit: Port Salut and mandarins or satsumas, Brie and freshly sliced apples, Camembert and pears, for instance. Allow about 100–150g (4–5oz) cheese per person. Arrange the cheese on a dark wooden serving

board and decorate with fruit. Serve with biscuits and butter.

In Between Courses
Surprise your guests at dinner, and serve cheese after the main course before the sweet dessert (in France cheese is usually served in this way). Allow about 150g (5oz) cheese per person. Serve rolls or coarse bread with the cheese.

Cheese and Wine
It is often difficult to choose the right wines for cheese, but here are some general rules:
Fresh cheeses (cream cheeses) – a dry, light white or rosé wine.

Brie or Camembert – a full-bodied red wine.
Blue cheeses (Roquefort, Stilton, Gorgonzola, etc) – a full-bodied red wine or port.
Hard cheeses (Emmenthal, Jarlsberg, Cheddar, Gouda, etc) – a dry white wine or a full-bodied red wine.

35

For the dough:
250g (9oz) strong, plain flour
15g (½oz) fresh yeast or 2 × level
   5ml tsp (2 level tsp) dried yeast
   plus 1 × 5ml tsp (1tsp) sugar
125ml (4½fl oz) lukewarm milk
   (hand-hot)
a pinch of salt
1 egg
25g (1oz) butter
For the filling:
200g (7oz) bacon or ham
2 small onions
4 eggs, separated
250ml (9fl oz) double cream
salt
2 × 15ml tbsp (2tbsp) finely chopped
   herbs (chives, parsley, dill,
   tarragon – one only, or a mixture)
250g (9oz) Swiss cheese, grated

1 Sieve the flour into the mixing bowl. Mix fresh yeast with the lukewarm milk, and mix into the flour. (If using dried yeast, dissolve the sugar in the warm milk, then the yeast, and leave for 10 min to get frothy. Then add to the flour.) Knead the dough thoroughly, for about 10 min, then sprinkle on a little flour and let the dough rise in a warm place for about 15 min.
2 Melt and cool the butter and work it into the dough together with the egg and salt. Knead the dough well and leave to rise again for about 15 min.
3 Roll out the dough and pat along the bottom and sides of the large, well-greased tin. Leave the dough to rise for a further 15 min.
4 Cut the bacon or ham in bite-sized pieces and spread them out on the pastry. Sauté chopped onions until slightly golden. Beat together egg yolks, cream and a little salt if used.
Add the finely chopped herbs, the sautéed onion, and the grated cheese. Beat the egg whites until stiff and fold them carefully into the mixture. Pour the batter into the lined tin, and bake in the preheated oven for 35–40 min.
Serve as a supper dish, alone or with a bowl of salad, and with red wine or beer.

Savoury Egg Pie, served with a salad, makes an excellent light lunch or supper.

From Oven to Table

Dishes like this are simple to serve. Everything else can be done while the dishes cook.

Cheese and Bacon Tart
(serves 4)
Preparation time: about 20 min
Cooking time for pastry: 1 hour
Baking time: 30–40 min
Oven temperature: 220°C, 425°F,
Gas 7
Suitable for the freezer but quality will be affected.

For the pastry:
200g (7oz) flour
150g (5oz) butter
3 × 15ml tbsp (3tbsp) water
For the filling:
200g (7oz) bacon or ham
250g (9oz) Swiss or Cheddar cheese
4 eggs
200ml (7fl oz) milk
pepper and salt if necessary
1 × 5ml tsp (1tsp) ground paprika
finely chopped parsley

1 Cut the butter into small pieces, and rub into the flour. Add cold water. Work the dough well together, then let it stand in a cold place for 30 min.
2 Roll out the pastry and line the bottom and the sides of a loose-bottomed flan tin. Leave to rest in the refrigerator for another 30 min.
3 Cut bacon or ham into cubes and fry them lightly. Finely grate the cheese. Spread the bacon cubes in the bottom of the pastry-lined flan tin and sprinkle cheese on top. Beat the eggs together with milk, pepper, salt, ground paprika and parsley, and pour the mixture into the pastry case. Bake the tart in the hot oven for about 30–40 min.
Serve piping hot with a bowl of salad, and red wine.

Savoury Egg Pie
(serves 4–6)
Round loose-bottomed baking tin, about 25cm (10in) in diameter
Preparation time: about 30 min
Dough rising time: 45 min
Baking time: 35–40 min
Oven temperature: 200°C, 400°F,
Gas 6
Unsuitable for the freezer

Savoury Egg Pie
1 Butter a large loose-bottomed tin, line with pastry dough and lay in the bacon pieces.

2 Whisk the egg yolks together with cream, herbs, onion and grated cheese, and fold in the egg-whites. Spoon the batter into the tin.

3 Bake the pie on the lowest rack for 35–40 min. Brown the sides by removing the baking tin, and slipping the pie back in the oven for a few minutes.

Egg and Vegetable Flan

(serves 4)

Flan tin, about 22cm (9in) in diameter

Preparation time: 15–20 min

Baking time: 45 min (in a pan of hot water)

Oven temperature: about 160–180°C, 325–350°F, Gas 3–4

Unsuitable for the freezer

3–4 small carrots
50g (2oz) butter
100g (4oz) mushrooms
1 leek
1 bay leaf, crushed
½ × 5ml tsp (¼tsp) dried or
*   1 × 5ml tsp (1tsp) fresh thyme*
8 eggs
50ml (2fl oz) double cream
100g (4oz) grated cheese (Cheddar
*   or Swiss)*
salt and pepper

1 Clean the carrots, cut them in thin slices and cook them for a few minutes in lightly salted water.

2 Clean the mushrooms and the leek, and sauté them for a few minutes in the butter, along with the thyme and bay leaf. Add the cooked carrot slices and pour the vegetable mixture into the greased flan tin.

3 Whisk the eggs lightly together with the cream. Add the grated cheese, salt and pepper and pour the mixture over the vegetables.

4 Place the flan tin in a baking tray of hot water, and bake for about 45 min.

Serve it with crisp French bread and butter and a salad.

Cheese and Ham Flan

(serves 6–8)

Flan tin, about 25cm (10in) in diameter

Baking time: 50 min

Oven temperature: 180°C, 350°F, Gas 4

Unsuitable for the freezer

For the dough :
250g (9oz) flour
175g (6oz) butter
100ml (4fl oz) cold water
¼ × 5ml tsp (¼tsp) salt
For the filling :
350g (¾lb) grated cheese (Jarlsberg,
*   Cheddar etc)*
200g (7oz) cooked ham, cubed
125g (4½oz) walnuts, finely chopped
5 eggs
400ml (¾pt) double cream
salt and pepper
fine breadcrumbs

1 Rub butter into flour with your fingertips and add water and salt. Work the dough until smooth and leave to chill for about 1 hour.

2 Roll out the dough and line the inside of the tin with it. Cover pastry with tinfoil and put in some baking beans. Bake this shell blind for about 20 min in the preheated oven on the lowest rack. Remove the tinfoil and beans.

3 Meanwhile, make the filling. Mix grated cheese with walnuts, add the lightly beaten eggs, and then the lightly whipped cream. Season and pour the batter and ham alternately into the tin. Sprinkle with breadcrumbs.

4 Continue baking the tart on the lowest rack at the same temperature for about 30 min and serve it piping hot.

Egg and Vegetable Flan (opposite)
and Cheese and Ham Flan (below),
both ideal served with French bread
and butter and a salad.

Quick Egg Meals

Chicken Soufflé (below)
(serves 4)
Preparation time: about 15 min
Baking time: 50–60 min (or 25 min)
Oven temperature: 200°C, 400°F,
Gas 6
Unsuitable for the freezer

25g (1oz) butter
3 × 15ml tbsp (3tbsp) flour
125ml (4½fl oz) chicken stock
125ml (4½fl oz) single cream
3 eggs, separated
250g (9oz) cooked chicken meat
150g (5oz) frozen peas
1 × 15ml tbsp (1tbsp) finely chopped
    parsley
1 × 15ml tbsp (1tbsp) chopped
    chervil
½ × 5ml tsp (½tsp) dried rosemary
a pinch of grated nutmeg
salt, pepper

1 Grease and flour a round soufflé
dish or 6–8 individual ramekins.
2 Remove the skin and bones from
the chicken, and cut the meat in
small cubes. Wash, dry and chop the
parsley and chervil.
3 Melt the butter in a saucepan, add
the flour and let it cook for a couple
of minutes without browning. Add
stock and cream and allow the sauce
to cook for a further few minutes.
Take the saucepan off the heat and
stir in the egg yolks, one at a time.
Whisk the egg whites until stiff.
4 Place chicken meat, peas, herbs,
nutmeg and seasoning into the
sauce. Fold in the egg whites. Pour
the batter into the well-greased and
floured baking dish or dishes.
5 Place in the oven immediately and
bake for 50–60 min (the individual
ramekins only need 25 min).

**Curried Eggs with
Cheese Sauce**
(serves 4)

4 hard-boiled eggs
3 × 15ml tbsp (3tbsp) mayonnaise
½ × 5ml tsp (½tsp) curry powder
2–3 × 5ml tsp (2–3tsp) finely
    chopped onion
½–1 × 15ml tbsp (½–1tbsp) finely
    chopped parsley
salt and pepper
For the sauce :
50g (2oz) butter
just over 25g (1oz) flour
¼ litre (18fl oz) milk
grated cheese
salt and pepper

1 Slice the hard-boiled eggs in two
lengthwise. Remove the yolks with a
teaspoon and mash them well together with mayonnaise, curry
powder, chopped onion and parsley.
Season with salt and pepper.
2 Fill the egg whites with the mixture and leave in a cold place for a
couple of hours.
3 Make the sauce and season it with
plenty of grated cheese.
4 Put the eggs in a greased baking
dish and pour the sauce over them.
Bake at 220°C, 425°F, Gas 7 for
about 10–15 min on the middle rack
of the oven.
Serve with individual rolls or
French bread and butter.

Eggs in Seafood Sauce (right)
(serves 4)

8 hard-boiled eggs
1 can mussels (in their own juice)
100g (4oz) cleaned shrimps
2 shallots or button onions
25–40g (1–1½oz) butter
1–1½ × 15ml tbsp (1–1½tbsp) flour
about 100ml (4fl oz) white wine or
    stock
100ml (4fl oz) double cream
curry powder (optional)
salt
pepper
finely chopped parsley

1 Melt the butter and sauté finely
chopped onions until transparent.
Stir in the flour, add the white wine
or stock with the juices from the
mussels gradually, and leave the
sauce to boil for a few minutes.
2 Add the cream, stir the sauce until
smooth, and season with salt, pepper
and curry powder (optional, but it
adds a nice flavour and delicate
colour). Add shrimps and mussels
and pour the sauce into a deep serving dish. Put the eggs on top and
sprinkle with parsley.
Serve the dish hot with lightly
cooked rice to which a dash of saf-
fron or turmeric has been added.

Egg and Cheese Canapés

Stuffed Eggs
(serves 4–8)

8 hard-boiled eggs
4 × 15ml tbsp (4tbsp) mayonnaise
2 × 15ml tbsp (2tbsp) double cream
celery salt
a pinch of white pepper
1 × 15ml tbsp (1tbsp) finely chopped
chives

Suggestions for garnishes :
slices of raw red pepper, pickled red
pepper, truffle, stuffed olive slices,
fillets of anchovy, small chunks of
sardine, tiny slices of ham, capers

1 Remove the shell from hard-boiled, chilled eggs and slice them in two lengthwise. Remove the egg yolks and press through a sieve.
2 Mix the sieved yolks with mayonnaise, cream, celery salt and pepper. Divide this mixture in two and add finely chopped chives to one half.

Two stuffed egg halves make a tasty
canapé or appetiser. Double the
portions and serve bread and a salad
as well for a simple supper dish.
From top to bottom : Cheese Éclairs,
Cheese Balls, Hot Cheese Tarts,
Cheese Cubes and Cheese Biscuits.

3 Fill the eggs with the yolk mixture with or without chives, and garnish according to your fancy.
Allow 2–4 half eggs per person, and the addition of fresh bread, butter, and a salad turns it into a simple supper dish.

Cheese Éclairs

250ml (9fl oz) water
65g (2½oz) butter
125g (4½oz) flour
3 eggs
100g (4oz) grated Swiss cheese
1 egg yolk
50g (2oz) grated cheese

1 Let the water come to a boil with the butter and then sprinkle in the flour. Work the mixture well together and leave to cook for a moment. Remove from the heat.
2 Stir in the eggs, one at a time, and continue stirring vigorously until the pastry comes away from the sides of the saucepan. Stir in the grated Swiss cheese.
3 Make small balls on a greased baking sheet with two spoons, or pipe them with an icing bag. Brush the balls with egg yolk and sprinkle them with more grated cheese. Bake in a hot oven (200°C, 400°F, Gas 6) for 20–25 min (do not open oven door during the first 10 min).

Cheese Balls

150g (5oz) cream cheese (plain or
  onion or garlic flavoured)
100g (4oz) butter
salt and pepper to taste
rye bread or pumpernickel
  breadcrumbs

1 Stir together cheese and butter and season with salt and pepper. Cool and roll out into small balls.
2 Roll the cheese balls in the dark breadcrumbs; stand in the refrigerator for 2hrs before serving.

Hot Cheese Tarts

200ml (7fl oz) thick, white sauce
1 chicken stock cube
2 eggs
50g (2oz) grated Swiss cheese
salt and cayenne pepper
nutmeg
about 225g (½lb) shortcrust frozen
  pastry, thawed
grated cheese

1 Make the filling first. Dissolve the stock cube in the hot sauce and remove the saucepan from the heat. Add the eggs, one at a time, and stir well between each addition. Add the cheese and stir until it has melted. Season and chill.
2 Roll the pastry out thinly. Line small tartlet tins or trays, prick the

pastry with a fork and fill with the thick sauce. Sprinkle a little grated cheese on top and bake the cheese tarts in a hot oven (200°C, 400°F, Gas 6). Serve piping hot.

Cheese Cubes

Swiss or Jarlsberg cheese
butter
finely chopped shelled walnuts

1 Cut the cheese in cubes and fry them carefully in a little butter, but not for too long. The cubes should be barely melted on the outside.
2 Roll the cheese cubes in the finely chopped walnuts. Fasten a grape onto each cheese cube with a wooden cocktail stick.

Cheese Biscuits

Small, salty biscuits
Edam cheese
red paprika
hot mustard

1 Cut the cheese in slices about 5mm (¼in) thick, and cut into triangles. Put the cheese and biscuits in layers with a tiny bit of mustard in between, and a piece of red pepper on top. Secure with cocktail stick.

Hot Appetisers

These are baked in the oven only until the cheese melts and the base is crisp and golden.

Pizza

For the basic pizza dough :
250g (9oz) flour
25g (1oz) fresh yeast, or 4 × level 5ml tsp (4 level tsp) dried yeast, plus 2 × 5ml tsp (2tsp) sugar
150ml (¼pt) hand-hot water
½ × 5ml tsp (½tsp) salt
2 × 15ml tbsp (2tbsp) oil

1 If using dried yeast, dissolve the sugar in the hand-hot water, then add the yeast and leave for 10 min to become frothy. Mix fresh yeast with the water. Mix all together into a smooth dough. Let it rise for about 20 min. Roll the dough out to a round about 35cm (14in) diameter and place on a greased baking sheet.
2 Spread the filling evenly over the flat round of dough, sprinkle with grated cheese and seasonings. Drip a little oil on the pizza. Bake for 12–15 min in a very hot oven (240°C, 475°F, Gas 9).

Pizza fillings
Simple Tomato Pizza

Spread a thin layer of tomato paste or purée on the rolled-out round of dough and place sliced tomatoes on top. Sprinkle salt and pepper on top, about 300g (11oz) grated Gruyère cheese and 1½–2 × 5ml tsp (1½–2tsp) pizza seasoning (oregano, marjoram, basil). Bake according to directions.

Anchovy Pizza

Cut 300g (11oz) Gruyère cheese into slices and spread them over the round of dough. Place 8 sliced tomatoes on top with anchovy fillets and half olives (optional). Sprinkle a little grated cheese over the filling and bake as described above.

Mushroom and Bacon Pizza

Skin 4–6 tomatoes, cut them in slices and sauté gently in 1½ × 15ml tbsp (1½tbsp) oil. Brush the rolled-out dough with 1½ × 15ml tbsp (1½tbsp) oil and spread the tomato mixture on top. Sprinkle over this 100g (4oz) grated Gruyère cheese, a little salt, pepper and oregano. Add sliced, fresh or canned mushrooms and 4–6 bacon rashers. When cooked, sprinkle finely chopped parsley on top.

Party Pizza (right)
(serves 4)

1 basic pizza dough
4 sliced tomatoes
½ red pepper
1 small can mushrooms
100g (4oz) shrimps
100g (4oz) salami or ham, sliced or in small chunks
8 black and 8 green stuffed olives
1 small can artichoke hearts (optional)
200g (7oz) grated Gruyère cheese
½–1 × 5ml tsp (½–1tsp) pizza seasoning (oregano, basil or thyme)
4 × 15ml tbsp (4tbsp) oil

Cut up the vegetables and spread all the ingredients on the pizza bottom. Stir together the pizza seasoning and oil and sprinkle over the filling. Bake in a fairly hot oven (220°C, 425°F, Gas 7) for 20–25 min.
Take the pizza out of the oven 10 min before the end of baking time, and sprinkle with the grated cheese. Continue baking until the cheese is melted and golden.

Open Toasted Cheese Sandwiches

These have infinite variations. Cut a few slices of bread, butter them and let your imagination be your guide (as well as anything you have left-over in the refrigerator).

Cheese Sandwich with Asparagus (left)
(serves 4)

about 450g (1lb) canned asparagus
4 slices square white bread
butter
4 thick slices of cooked ham
4 thick slices of Gruyère or Emmenthal cheese
about 1 × 15ml tbsp (1tbsp) chopped chives

1 Drain the asparagus well. Toast the slices of bread and butter them. Place the slices of ham on top, then the asparagus and finally a slice of cheese.
2 Place the slices of bread in a hot oven or under the grill and leave them until the cheese melts. Sprinkle the sandwiches with finely chopped chives and serve immediately.

Blinis – a Delicious Appetiser

Blinis are small pancakes which originate from Russia, where they are served with real caviar. More economically, serve them – hot or cold – with sour cream or whipped double cream and Danish caviar (lumpfish roe). Allow two per person.

(serves 4)

15g (½oz) yeast, or 2 × 5ml tsp
   (2tsp) dried yeast, plus
   ½ × 5ml tsp (½tsp) sugar

150ml (¼pt) hand-hot milk
150ml (¼pt) Pils or lager beer
1 egg, separated
150g (5oz) flour
1 × 5ml tsp (1tsp) salt
2 × 15ml tbsp (2tbsp) double cream

Garnishes :
100g (4oz) Danish caviar (lumpfish
   roe)
150ml (¼pt) double or sour cream
1 × 15ml tbsp (1tbsp) finely chopped
   chives or onion

1 Dissolve the fresh yeast in luke-warm milk. If using dried yeast, dis-solve the sugar in the milk, add the yeast, and leave 10 min to become frothy. Mix into the flour, stirring all the while. Let it rise for an hour.

2 Add the beer, egg yolk, salt and cream, stir well and let the mixture stand in a warm place to rise for further 30–40 min.

3 Beat the egg whites stiff and fold them carefully into the batter. After the egg whites have been added, the blinis must be fried immediately.

4 Warm a little butter in a small frying pan (preferably iron) about 12–14cm (5–6in) in diameter.

5 Fry the blinis over low heat until golden brown and porous. Pile them on top of each other as they are finished.

6 Serve the blinis freshly made with lightly whipped cream or sour cream, caviar and chopped chives or onion.

Everyday and Party Pancakes

If you want paper-thin pancakes which melt in the mouth, it's best to use as little flour as possible – and plenty of eggs.

NB Pancakes can be frozen without the filling. Pile them on top of one another, with greaseproof paper between each layer.

Basic Pancake Batter
(makes 12)

4 eggs
150g (5oz) flour
a pinch of salt
200ml (7fl oz) milk
200ml (7fl oz) single cream
25g (1oz) melted butter

Double pancakes with a filling are a good and satisfying main course. See recipes on pages 51 and 52.

1 Put flour, salt, half of the milk and the eggs in a bowl. Beat vigorously until you get a smooth, thick batter. Add the rest of the milk, the cream and the butter and stir well. Let the batter stand in a cool place for at least 1 hr.
2 Butter the frying pan well and fry the pancakes over low to medium heat on both sides.

Pancakes Filled with Creamed Mushrooms (above)
(serves 4)

4 pancakes
For the filling:
250g (9oz) cleaned button mushrooms
15g ($\frac{1}{2}$oz) butter
salt and pepper
finely chopped parsley
2 × 5ml tsp (2tsp) flour
400ml ($\frac{3}{4}$pt) single cream

Sauté the mushrooms in the butter. (If they're large, slice them first.) Sprinkle the flour on top, and add salt and pepper to taste. Add cream and continue stirring until you have a smooth creamy mixture. Stir in finely chopped parsley. Spread the filling on 4 pancakes, fold them carefully together, or roll them up and decorate with a sprig of parsley.

49

Family-favourite Pancakes
(serves 4)

8 pancakes
For the filling :
450–550g (1–1¼lb) minced beef
butter
1 large onion
1 red or green pepper
1 celery stalk
2 × 15ml tbsp (2tbsp) tomato paste
150ml (¼pt) water
1 beef stock cube
paprika, salt, pepper
a pinch of sugar
basil and grated nutmeg
grated cheese

1 Fry the minced beef in a little butter until it is brown. Add chopped pepper, onion and celery and let it all simmer until the vegetables are tender. Add the tomato paste, water and stock cube and season with the paprika, salt, pepper, sugar, basil and grated nutmeg. Let it all simmer, covered, over a low heat for at least 30 min (preferably longer).
2 Spread the filling over the pancakes and roll them up as in the photograph above. Serve them as they are, or place them in a buttered baking dish, sprinkle grated cheese on top and bake in a hot oven (220°C, 425°F, Gas 7) 10–15 min.

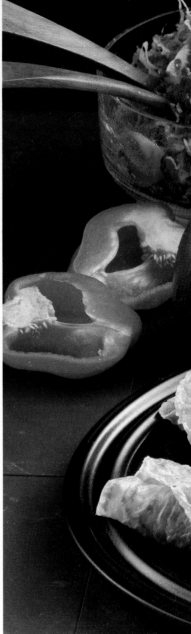

Shrimp Pancakes (left)
(serves 4)

8 pancakes
For the filling :
300g (11oz) cleaned shrimps
40g (1½oz) butter
1 × 15ml tbsp (1tbsp) finely chopped
  dill
250ml (9fl oz) sour cream
salt, pepper, lemon juice
50g (2oz) grated Swiss cheese
finely chopped parsley

1 Melt the butter in the frying pan and add shrimps, chopped dill and

half the sour cream. Let it all simmer on a gentle heat for a couple of minutes. Season with salt, pepper and lemon juice.

2 Spread the filling over the pancakes and roll them up as in the photograph. Put the pancakes tightly together in a buttered baking dish. Spread the rest of the sour cream over the pancakes and sprinkle the grated cheese on top.

3 Bake the rolled pancakes in a hot oven (220°C, 425°F, Gas 7) for about 15 min. Sprinkle finely chopped parsley on top and serve the dish hot with a green salad.

Double Cheese Pancakes
(serves 4)

8 pancakes
For the filling :
butter
100g (4oz) grated Parmesan cheese
100g (4oz) grated Swiss cheese
8 × 15ml tbsp (8tbsp) double cream

1 Put a little butter in the frying pan and place it over a low heat. Place a pancake in the frying pan, sprinkle a couple of tablespoons of each of the types of cheese on top, and add a little cream. Brush around the edge

Family-favourite Pancakes with a substantial meat filling.

with a little left-over pancake batter. Place the second pancake on top of the first and press them carefully together around the edge. Fry the pancake for only about 1–2 min on each side (turn them over with a large fish slice, or by turning them onto a plate, and then sliding them back in again, other side up).

Decorate with tomato wedges and parsley and serve hot, with soup for a light, delicious, lunch.

Pancake Omelettes with Veal Fricassée (above)
(serves 4)

8 × 15ml tbsp (8tbsp) flour
6 eggs
300ml (½pt) milk
salt and white pepper
butter for frying
For the filling:
450g (1lb) boned veal
1 large onion
25g (1oz) butter
1 × 15ml tbsp (1tbsp) flour
250ml (9fl oz) chicken or veal stock
125ml (4½fl oz) asparagus juice
  (from the can, see below)
1 × level 5ml tsp (1 level tsp) salt
white pepper
a pinch of grated nutmeg
25g (1oz) thawed frozen peas
1 small can asparagus chunks
1 small can mushrooms
2 × 15ml tbsp (2tbsp) double cream
1 egg yolk

1 Prepare the filling first. Chop the onion finely and let it sauté in butter until soft and golden.
2 Cut the veal in cubes and let it fry with the onion, without browning, for about 10 min. Sprinkle the flour on top and gradually add the stock and juice from the can of asparagus. Season with salt, pepper and nutmeg, and let simmer for about 30 min or until the meat is tender.
3 Add peas, the well-drained asparagus chunks and drained mushrooms, and heat everything in the sauce. Stir together the cream and the egg yolk and add to the meat sauce. Do not let the sauce boil after the egg yolk has been added.

Pancake omelettes
1 Sift the flour into a bowl. Make a well in the centre, add the eggs, and beat well. Add milk, salt and pepper and beat until the batter is smooth and free of lumps.
2 Melt a little butter in the frying-pan and fry 4 pancake omelettes on both sides.
3 Fill them with the veal sauce and decorate with a sprig of parsley.

Oven Pancake with Pork
(serves 4)

150g (5oz) flour
a pinch of salt
800ml (28fl oz) milk
4 eggs
40g (1½oz) butter
200g (7oz) smoked belly pork or
  ham
finely chopped parsley

1 Mix flour and salt in a bowl. Make a well in the centre, add the milk a little at a time, and beat until the batter is smooth and free of lumps. Beat in the eggs and let the batter rest for at least 1 hr.
2 Cut the pork or ham in cubes and fry in butter until crisp and brown. Place in a buttered oven dish and pour the pancake batter over.
3 Bake the oven pancake (220°C, 425°F, Gas 7) for 30–40 min or until it has a nice golden colour. Cut the pancake into pieces, sprinkle parsley on top and serve with cranberry jam or a green salad.

Rolled Salmon Pancake
(serves 4)

3 large eggs
300ml (½pt) water
100g (4oz) flour
1 × 5ml tsp (1tsp) baking powder
a pinch of salt
300ml (½pt) milk
For the filling :
200–300g (7–11oz) smoked salmon
  in paper-thin slices
butter
fresh dill

1 Beat the eggs and add water, flour mixed with baking powder, and salt. Beat thoroughly until the batter is smooth and free of lumps. Add the milk and beat well.
2 Butter an oven dish well and pour in the batter. Bake the pancake (220°C, 425°F, Gas 7) until firm and a nice golden colour, about 20–30 min.
3 Heat the slices of salmon in a little butter in a pan and place them on top of the pancake. Sprinkle with plenty of finely chopped dill and roll up the pancake like a Swiss roll. Cut into thick slices and serve with a green salad.

Seafood Pancakes (above)
(serves 4)

250g (9oz) flour
a pinch of salt
4 eggs
500ml (about 1pt) milk
2 × 15ml tbsp (2tbsp) melted butter
butter for frying
For the filling :
25g (1oz) butter
2 × 15ml tbsp (2tbsp) flour
350ml (12–13fl oz) creamy milk
½ chicken stock cube
1 small onion
1 sprig of parsley
1 egg yolk
salt, white pepper
200g (7oz) cleaned shrimps, or
  crabmeat

1 Sift the flour into a bowl and add the salt. Make a well in the centre, and stir in the milk and eggs, a little at a time, so that the batter is smooth and free of lumps. Add the butter.
2 Put the butter for frying in the frying pan and fry the pancakes over low heat on both sides. Keep them hot while you make the filling.
3 Melt butter, stir in flour and add the creamy milk gradually. Add the half stock cube and stir until dissolved. Chop the parsley and onion finely and fry separately in butter until soft. Add to the sauce and let it simmer for about 10 min.
4 Remove the sauce from the heat. Beat 1 egg yolk together with a couple of tablespoons of the sauce and pour it back into the sauce, beating all the while. The sauce must not cook after the egg yolk has been added. Add the shrimps or crabmeat at the very end and season the filling with salt and pepper.
5 Put 2–3 × 15ml tbsp (2–3tbsp) of the filling on each pancake and fold together. Serve the pancakes piping hot, garnished with lettuce, slices of tomato and fresh dill.

53

Dessert Pancakes

Pancakes make a light and delicious dessert, served individually with a filling, or as one large cake.

Tosca Pancakes (above)
(serves 4)

pancake batter (see basic recipe, this page)
For the filling:
5 apples
about 300ml (½pt) orange juice
For the topping:
1½ × 15ml tbsp (1½tbsp) clear honey

about 100–125g (4–4½oz) sugar
75g (3oz) butter
75g (3oz) blanched, sliced almonds
1 × 15ml tbsp (1tbsp) flour
1 × 15ml tbsp (1tbsp) milk

1 Peel the apples, halve them, and quarter the halves. Put them into the orange juice mixed with a little water.
2 Fry thin pancakes and put them in layers with the drained apple sections in a baking dish. Begin with a pancake and finish off with a pancake.
3 Mix the topping ingredients in a saucepan and let them come to a boil, stirring all the while.
4 Pour over the pile of pancakes and put the dish into a pre-heated hot oven (220°C, 425°F, Gas 7) until

the 'cake' is a nice golden colour. Decorate further with apple or mandarin sections, or fresh berries.

Basic Dessert Pancakes
(makes about 12)

4 eggs
100g (4oz) flour
800ml (28fl oz) milk
butter for frying

1 Make a well in the flour, and beat in a little milk gradually until the batter is free of lumps.
2 Add the eggs and the remaining milk and let the batter rest in a cold place.
3 Fry thin pancakes in butter. Lay them on top of each other as they are fried.

Pancakes with Strawberries and Cream
(per person)

1 pancake
50ml (2fl oz) double cream or 50ml
(2fl oz) cottage cheese and 25ml
(1fl oz) double cream
6–8 fresh strawberries
grated chocolate

Fill the pancake with whipped cream or a mixture of cream and cottage cheese, and decorate with strawberries and chocolate.

Pancakes with Cherries
(per person)

2 pancakes
4 × 15ml tbsp (4tbsp) canned
cherries with a little juice
2 × 5ml tsp (2tsp) orange liqueur

Heat the cherries without cooking them and stir in the orange liqueur. Put the mixture on top of the pancakes, fold them in two or four and decorate with a thin slice of orange.

Pancakes with Peaches
(per person)

1 pancake
2 canned peaches
1 × 15ml tbsp (1tbsp) white rum
1–2 × 15ml tbsp (1–2tbsp) cranberry
jam
toasted, sliced almonds

Cut the peaches into sections and lay them on top of the pancake. Stir the cranberries and rum together and spread over the peaches. Sprinkle almonds on top.

Pancakes with Pineapple
(per person)

1–2 pancakes
1–2 rings of canned pineapple
a few canned cherries
2–3 × 15ml tbsp (2–3tbsp) chocolate
sauce
coarsely chopped almonds or
pistachios

Cut the pineapple rings into pieces and mix them with the well-drained cherries. Fill the pancakes with the mixture, pour over the chocolate sauce, and sprinkle with the coarsley chopped nuts.

1 Let the raisins soak in the rum for about 30 min. Take them out, and drain them well.

2 Beat the egg yolks, salt and sugar together until white and thick. Stir in the milk, left-over rum and flour (with the vanilla sugar) alternately. Add the raisins. Beat the egg whites stiff and fold them into the batter.

3 Melt 15g ($\frac{1}{2}$oz) butter in a frying-pan (about 20cm or 8in in diameter). Pour half the batter into the frying pan and fry the pancake over low heat for 5–6 min, or until golden. Turn the pancake over (use a well-buttered plate), put it back into the pan and fry the other side.

4 Divide the 'pancake' into small pieces (see photograph left) with 2 forks. Keep them warm. Fry the rest of the batter in the same way. Finally, put all the pancake pieces into the frying-pan with a little butter and heat them for a couple of minutes over low heat. Put the pancake pieces onto a warm serving dish and sift icing sugar on top.

Serve the pieces of pancake as a dessert with some good jam, or some lightly whipped cream.

Cream Pancakes
(serves 4)

300ml ($\frac{1}{2}$pt) double cream
2 × 15ml tbsp (2tbsp) flour
3 egg yolks
a pinch of salt
2 egg whites
butter for frying

1 Whip the cream until stiff. Stir in flour, egg yolks and salt. Beat the egg whites stiff and fold them in.

2 Melt a little butter in the frying pan for each pancake you fry. Use a smallish frying pan, and fry these pancakes on one side only.

3 Lay the pancakes in pairs, with the uncooked sides together, with a little jam in the middle.

Sour Cream Pancakes
(serves 4)

2 eggs
300ml ($\frac{1}{2}$pt) sour cream
2 × 15ml tbsp (2tbsp) flour
1 × 5ml tsp (1tsp) vanilla sugar (see page 25)
1 × 5ml tsp (1tsp) sugar

1 Separate the eggs. Beat the whites stiff, and mix flour with the two

Pancakes with a Difference

For dessert or with your coffee.

Dessert Pancakes (above)
(serves 4)

2 × 15ml tbsp (2tbsp) raisins
4 × 15ml tbsp (4tbsp) white rum
4 egg yolks
3 × 15ml tbsp (3tbsp) sugar
a pinch of salt
500ml (18fl oz) milk
100g (4oz) flour
1 × 5ml tsp (1tsp) vanilla sugar (see page 25)
5 egg whites
butter for frying
icing sugar

sugars. Mix the egg yolks and the sour cream carefully into the egg whites, and then mix in the flour.

2 Butter a small frying pan well and fry small pancakes on both sides. Serve the pancakes hot with jam, berries or soft fruit, or with a little tinned fruit and a blob of whipped cream.

Swiss Deep-fried Pancakes
(makes about 20)

5 eggs
25g (1oz) sugar
a pinch of salt
50g (2oz) butter
5 × 15ml tbsp (5tbsp) double cream
500g (1lb 2oz) flour
500g (1lb 2oz) lard, for deep-frying

1 Beat the eggs, sugar and salt well together. Melt the butter. Mix the butter and cream into the eggs. Sift in the flour and work the dough well together until it comes away from the side of the bowl. Wrap the dough in a damp dish-towel and leave in a cool place for at least an hour.

2 Divide the dough into small pieces and shape them into balls. Roll out the balls into paper-thin round pancakes, about the size of a side plate.

3 Heat the lard until smoking hot. Deep-fry the pancakes until light golden on both sides. Drain them well on paper towels. Sift a little icing sugar on top and serve them with coffee. Photograph on right.

Rice Pancakes
(serves 4)

3 eggs
1 × 15ml tbsp (1tbsp) sugar
100g (4oz) rice pudding
100g (4oz) flour
1 × 5ml tsp (1tsp) vanilla sugar (see page 25)
½ × 5ml tsp (½tsp) salt
butter for frying

1 Beat eggs and sugar together thoroughly. First mix in the rice-pudding, then the flour, to which has been added vanilla sugar and salt.

2 Melt butter in an ordinary or small frying pan and fry small, round pancakes on both sides. Serve the pancakes hot with sugar or jam.

Simple Pancakes
(serves 4)

2 eggs
150g (5oz) flour
600ml (1pt) milk
½ × 5ml tsp (½tsp) salt
½ × 15ml tbsp (½tbsp) sugar
butter for frying

1 Beat together the eggs and some of the milk. Add the flour and beat to a smooth, even batter. Mix in the rest of the milk, salt and sugar and beat well.

Let the batter rest for at least 1 hour, or preferably overnight in a cold place.

2 Melt a little butter in a small frying pan. Fry small pancakes on both sides. Serve the pancakes hot, with fresh jam.

Baked Custard with Shrimps

1 Sauté shrimp shells and vegetables in butter.

2 Add stock and wine and simmer over low heat for about 15 min.

3 Beat the eggs and the cooled milk together, then add shrimp stock.

Baked Custards in Ring Moulds

Baked custard is both easy and delicious. You can make it well in advance, even the day before you intend to serve it. The filling can be partially or wholly ready and only needs warming up before serving. Choose any filling you fancy – fish, seafood, ham, mushrooms, vegetables...

Baked Custard with Shrimps
(serves 4–5)
Use a circular ring mould (about $1\frac{1}{2}$ litres or $2\frac{1}{2}$pt)
Baking time: 30 min
Oven temperature: 160°C, 325°F, Gas 3
Unsuitable for the freezer

For the shrimp stock :
2 × 15ml tbsp (2tbsp) butter
shrimp shells (see below)
2 shallots or button onions
celery stalk
$\frac{1}{2}$ leek
200ml (7fl oz) chicken stock (water + cube)
200ml (7fl oz) dry white wine
For the custard :
6 eggs
200ml (7fl oz) milk
100ml (4fl oz) shrimp stock
 For the sauce :
200ml (7fl oz) shrimp stock
200ml (7fl oz) double cream

15g ($\frac{1}{2}$oz) butter
1 × 15ml tbsp (1tbsp) flour
400g (14oz) shrimps

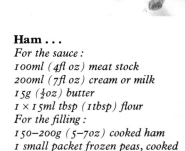

1 To make the stock, peel the shrimps and chop up the vegetables. Sauté the shrimp shells and vegetables in butter.
2 Add the chicken stock and wine gradually. Let it come to a boil and simmer over low heat for about 15 min. Strain the mixture.
3 To make the custard, let the milk come to a boil and then cool it. Beat the eggs together and then add the milk. Add 100ml (4fl oz) of the shrimp stock.
4 Pour the custard into the well-buttered ring mould. Cover it with tinfoil and bake in a pan of water in the preheated oven for about 30 min. Set the mould aside to cool.
5 To make the sauce, simmer the rest of the shrimp stock with the cream, and add balls of butter and flour mixed together. Stir until the sauce is smooth and even.
6 Season it with a little salt and pepper, some lemon juice (optional) and mix in the cleaned shrimps.
7 Loosen the custard with a knife and turn it out onto a platter. Pile the shrimps and sauce into the centre. Garnish with some fresh lettuce leaves, sections of orange and a little fresh dill.
Serve with crisp white bread or individual rolls, butter and a glass of white wine or beer.

VARIATIONS
You can vary the fillings in the centre of the custard, but you must replace the fishy stock with milk and/or cream.

Ham ...
For the sauce :
100ml (4fl oz) meat stock
200ml (7fl oz) cream or milk
15g ($\frac{1}{2}$oz) butter
1 × 15ml tbsp (1tbsp) flour
For the filling :
150–200g (5–7oz) cooked ham
1 small packet frozen peas, cooked

Mushrooms ...
For the sauce :
100ml (4fl oz) stock from canned mushrooms (or vegetable stock)
200ml (7fl oz) cream/milk
15g ($\frac{1}{2}$oz) butter
1 × 15ml tbsp (1tbsp) flour
For the filling :
250g (9oz) fresh mushrooms (or equivalent weight of canned)

Sauté the mushrooms briefly in butter and mix them into the sauce.

4 Make sauce with stock, cream, adding balls of butter and flour.

5 Season the sauce and add the cleaned shrimps.

6 Loosen the custard with a knife and turn it out onto a platter.

Cocottes with Variations
... with Spinach
(per person)

50g (2oz) frozen creamed spinach
25g (1oz) butter
2–3 × 15ml tbsp (2–3tbsp) cream
a pinch of salt
1 egg

Thaw the spinach and put it in a buttered ramekin, dot with butter and add the cream. Sprinkle on a little salt and drop the egg into a little hollow in the middle. Bake the ramekin in the oven (200°C, 400°F, Gas 6) for 10–15 min until the dish is heated through and the white of the egg has set.

... with 'Caviar'
(per person)

2 × 15ml tbsp (2tbsp) finely chopped onion
2 × 15ml tbsp (2tbsp) lumpfish roe
1 × 15ml tbsp (1tbsp) lemon juice
finely chopped parsley
½ × 15ml tbsp (½tbsp) olive oil
1 egg

Mix all the ingredients together (except the egg) and place them in a circle in the ramekin. Drop the egg in the middle and bake as directed above.

... with Seafood and Asparagus
(per person)

2 × 15ml tbsp (2tbsp) asparagus tips
2 × 15ml tbsp (2tbsp) shrimps or mussels
15g (½oz) butter
2 × 15ml tbsp (2tbsp) cream
a pinch of salt

Smiling Eggs
(serves 4)

200g (7oz) mayonnaise
about 100ml (4fl oz) buttermilk
salt, pepper, lemon juice
grated onion
dry mustard and a pinch of curry
*   powder*
1 bunch radishes, finely chopped
3–4 × 15ml tbsp (3–4tbsp) finely
*   chopped parsley*
8 pilchards
4–6 eggs, boiled for 7–8 min

Mix all ingredients except pilchards and eggs. Pour the sauce into a shallow platter and put the pilchards and eggs on top.

Hard-boiled Eggs with Bacon
(serves 4–6)

8–12 hard-boiled eggs, shelled
450g (1lb) packet frozen chips, or
*   4–5 potatoes, cubed and fried*
100g (4oz) bacon
1 red pepper
For the sauce :
25–40g (1–1½oz) butter
2 × 15ml tbsp (2tbsp) flour
500ml (just under 1pt) milk
salt

Make the sauce and pour it into a deep serving dish. Put whole, boiled eggs, fried potatoes, crisply fried bacon rashers and pepper on top.

white pepper
1 egg

Arrange the asparagus and seafood in an individual ramekin, or larger dish as in the photograph. Dot with butter and pour cream on top. Season and drop the egg in the middle. Bake as directed above.

Clockwise from the back left of the large picture : Hard-boiled Eggs with Bacon, Smiling Eggs, 'Caviar' and Spinach Cocottes. Right : Seafood and Asparagus Cocottes.

Tasty Hot Dishes

So often left-overs can be combined with a few eggs to make delicious hot dishes.

Egg and Vegetable Bake
   (below)
(serves 4–5)

150–250g (5–9oz) bacon
butter and oil
450g (1lb) onions
2–3 red or green peppers
about 450g (1lb) firm tomatoes
1 × 5ml tsp (1tsp) dried basil or
   oregano
salt and pepper
6 eggs
finely chopped parsley

1 Fry the bacon and put it aside in a warm place.
2 Sauté sliced onion in the bacon fat, with a little butter or oil, until transparent. Add coarsely chopped or sliced peppers, sliced tomatoes, and dried herb. Sauté over low heat until soft. Season to taste.
3 Pour beaten eggs on top and stir a little until the egg mixture becomes firm.
Serve the bacon on top of or beside the dish and sprinkle parsley on top. Serve with bread and butter, and with a simple selection of cheeses afterwards, you have a filling meal.

Cheesy Ham and Leeks
(serves 4)

4 eggs
4 × 15ml tbsp (4tbsp) water
½ × 5ml tsp (½tsp) salt
100g (4oz) grated cheese (Cheddar)
2 slices cooked ham
2 × 15ml tbsp (2tbsp) finely chopped
   leeks
25g (1oz) butter

1 Beat the eggs lightly together with water and salt. Brown the butter a little in the pan and pour the egg mixture in. Sprinkle all the cheese on top and lay strips of leek and ham over the cheese.
2 Cover the pan with a lid, or with doubled tinfoil, and let it cook over medium heat for 5–6 minutes.
The dish is ready when it is golden in colour and the egg mixture firm. Serve as a light lunch with soup as a first course or as a hot supper. Serve with freshly baked rolls or French bread and butter.

Supper Dish with Left-overs
(serves 4)

225–350g (½–¾lb) left-over ham,
   bacon or sausage
1 onion
3–4 boiled potatoes
4 eggs
4–6 × 15ml tbsp (4–6tbsp) water
½ × 5ml tsp (½tsp) salt

1 Cut the meat and potatoes into small cubes, chop the onion coarsely and brown together in the frying-pan.

2 Beat the eggs, water and salt lightly together and pour it over the meat and vegetables in the pan. Lift the egg mixture a little so that the egg sets gradually like an omelette. Sprinkle chopped parsley on top. The dish may also be made in a baking dish and baked in the oven (about 180°C, 350°F, Gas 4) until ready.

Left-over Casserole (above)
Left-overs of cooked fish, seafood and cooked vegetables are used in this colourful dish. Cooked long-grain rice makes the dish go further and adds to the flavour.

1 Butter a lidded casserole or baking dish and put in cooked rice,

lightly cooked pieces of celery or green beans, fish and a few poached shrimps or other seafood. Sprinkle a little pepper and salt between the layers. Put the lid on and bake in a hot oven until everything is thoroughly heated.

2 Meanwhile, beat 3–4 egg whites very stiff with a little salt, or stir 2 egg yolks with 8 × 15ml tbsp (8tbsp) mayonnaise and fold in 2 stiffly beaten egg whites. Remove the baking dish from the oven and spread the egg mixture over the top. Put the baking dish into the oven again and let it bake until the surface is golden.

Cheese Casserole
(serves 4)
Preparation time: about 20 min
Baking time: about 20 min
Oven temperature: 200°C, 400°F, Gas 6

1 small cauliflower
1 leek
4 eggs
4 × 15ml tbsp (4tbsp) water
1 × 5ml tsp (1tsp) salt
150g (5oz) cheese (Cheddar, Swiss or Jarlsberg)

1 Chop up the vegetables and cook them until almost tender in lightly salted water.

2 Butter a casserole or baking dish and put in the vegetables. Beat the eggs lightly together with water and salt and pour the mixture over the vegetables.

3 Sprinkle grated cheese on top and put the baking dish into a pre-heated hot oven for about 20 min until the surface is an attractive golden colour. Serve with rolls and butter.

Index

Using Templates

Each puppet is made with felt shapes which have to be cut out before you can start sticking.

First, read the puppet instructions to see which template shapes you need, then find them on page 32.

Use tracing paper and a pencil to transfer the template shapes onto a piece of white paper, then cut them out.*

Finally, choose the colours of felt you need and ask an adult to pin the paper templates on, and cut carefully around the edges. (You could do this all by yourself if you're confident.)

TOP TIP

• If you don't have felt in the colours you need, choose from your own selection.
• Keep your paper templates somewhere safe, so you can use them again.
• When your puppet is finished, carefully push a pencil into the finger hole and leave the glue to dry overnight.
• Don't use finger puppets before they are dry, or they may fall apart.

* You'll need to cut out your own felt shapes for most of the ears, noses and paws, as these are tiny and easier to create for yourself. Make sure they are the right size to fit your puppet.

You will need
• 2 x goggle eyes
• A black pen
• Felt: brown, red, yellow and orange
• Glue

Cock-a-doodle-doooo!

4

FINGER PUPPETS
Craft Book

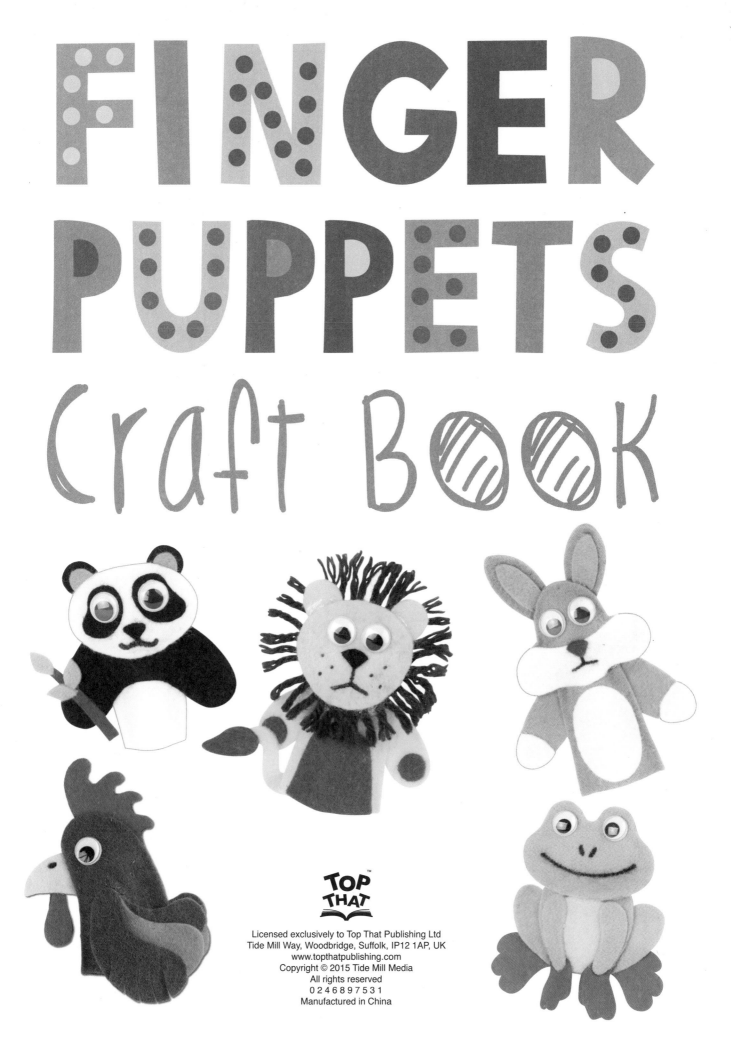

TOP THAT™

Licensed exclusively to Top That Publishing Ltd
Tide Mill Way, Woodbridge, Suffolk, IP12 1AP, UK
www.topthatpublishing.com
Copyright © 2015 Tide Mill Media
0 2 4 6 8 9 7 5 3 1
Manufactured in China

Getting Started

Finger puppets are cute, cool and fun! To make the collection of characters in this book, just follow the step-by-step instructions and use the pattern templates on page 32 to get started.

Items you'll need

You can buy everything you need from craft and hobby shops, or online. The main items you'll need are felt in different colours, goggle eyes, fabric glue and a black pen. You'll need a few other items too, plus a pair of scissors for every project.

Instead of buying goggle eyes, you could make your own using circles of white and black card.

Check out the list at the beginning of each project and gather everything together before you start, so you're ready to get making straight away!

Making a mess

Although making a mess sounds like fun, it's not a good way to make neat finger puppets. So, before you start:
• Cover your working area with old newspaper.
• If you get glue on your fingers, stop and wash your hands.
• Keep spare scraps of felt as they may be useful later for small parts, such as ears, noses and paws.

Cock-a-doodle Cockerel

You can make great noises for this puppet as he sits on your finger!

Template pieces:
- Body A (cut 2 from brown felt)
- Beak A (cut 2 from yellow felt)
- Wing A (cut 2 from brown felt)
- Comb (cut 1 from red felt)
- Wing B (cut 2 from orange felt)
- Wattle (cut 2 from red felt)
- Wing C (cut 2 from brown felt)

Cock-a-doodle-doo!

Cluck! Cluck!

1 Glue one side of the beak and place the two wattle pieces on the bottom edge.

Press the other side of the beak on top to hold the wattle pieces in place.

Be careful when you use the glue. It can be very messy!

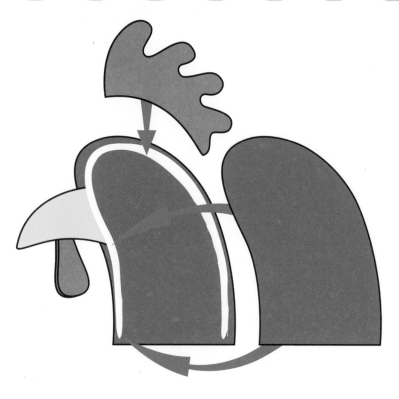

2 Glue carefully around the edges of one body shape, leaving the bottom (flat) edge unglued. Put the beak at the front edge and press firmly. Position the comb on top of the head and press down.

3 Add more glue where the beak and comb have covered up the glue around the edge. Stick the other body shape on top to hold everything in place.

4 Put a big dot of glue on the narrow end of a wing C piece and stick wing B on top, just overlapping. Glue the bottom edge of wing B and stick wing A on top in the same way.

5 Repeat step 4 to make the second wing. Carefully snip the bottom part of each of the two wing A pieces to look like a feathery edge.

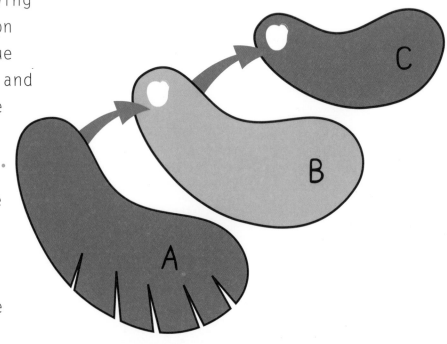

6 Glue a wing to each side of the cockerel's body, about half way up.

7 Add a goggle eye on each side of the cockerel and leave the puppet overnight to dry properly. Finish the cockerel by drawing a small black mark on each side of his beak.

You will need
• 2 x goggle eyes
• Brown wool
• A black pen
• Glue
• Felt: yellow,
brown and black

Little Lost Lion

This little fellow may be grown-up enough to have a great mane, but he looks a bit scared and lost!

Template pieces:
- Body B (cut 2 from yellow felt)
- Head A (cut 2 from yellow felt)
- Tummy A (cut 1 from brown felt)
- Arm B (cut 2 from yellow felt)
- Tail A (cut 1 from yellow felt)
- Tail B (cut 1 from brown felt)

Cut your own:
- Ear (cut 2 from yellow felt)
- Nose (cut 1 from black felt)
- Paw (cut 2 from brown felt)

1   Glue an arm at each side of one body piece. Glue all around the body, except the bottom edge, and stick the other body piece on top. Leave to dry under a heavy book.

2 Glue the whole of one head piece and cut your wool into lots of 2 cm pieces. Position the wool pieces around the edge of the head piece, meeting under the chin.

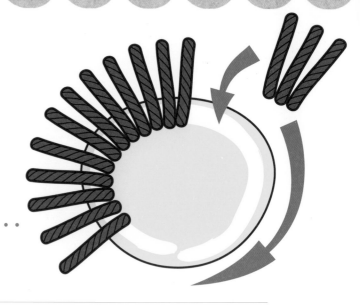

3 Glue the ears behind the top of the other head piece. Spread glue all over the back of this head piece and stick it on top of the other head section.

4 Stick the nose in the middle of the face. Draw on a mouth and whisker spots. Stick on the goggle eyes.

5 Stick the tummy onto the front of the body section. Glue the paws to the ends of the arms, too.

. . . .

6 Add glue to the very top of the body, above the tummy, and stick the head in place.

. . . .

7 Turn the puppet over. Glue tail A in place at the bottom of the back. Turn the puppet the right way round again to glue tail B in place at the end. Leave to dry overnight.

You will need
• 2 x Goggle eyes
• A black pen
• Felt: white, black, green, brown and pink
• Glue

12

Happy Panda

Pandas are one of the world's most endangered species, but this happy panda is still smiling!

Template pieces:
- Body D (cut 2 from white felt)
- Head B (cut 1 from white felt)
- Arm C (cut 2 from black felt)
- Eye (cut 2 from black felt)

Cut your own:
- Nose (cut 1 from black felt)
- Inner ear (cut 2 from pink felt)
- Leaf (cut 3 from green felt)
- Outer ear (cut 2 from black felt)
- Bamboo Cane (cut 1 from brown felt)

1 Glue carefully around the edge of one body part, leaving a gap at the bottom. Stick the other part on top and press the edges together firmly.

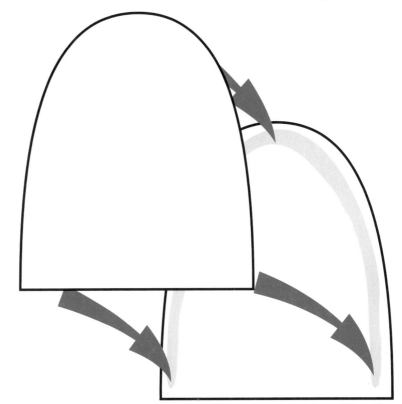

2 Glue one arm piece at the top of the body. This is now the front of your panda.

3 Glue the bamboo cane in place at the end of one arm. Stick the leaves at the top.

4 Glue the felt eyes in place on the panda's head. Stick the goggle eyes on top. Glue on the nose and draw the panda's mouth.

5 Stick the head at the top of the body and arms. Now turn the whole puppet over.

6 Glue the other arm piece in place at the top of the body. Make sure the ends are glued to the front arm piece.

7 Glue the inner ears to the outer ears. Stick each ear in place at the top of the panda's head, on the back. Leave the puppet to dry overnight.

Wide-mouthed Frog

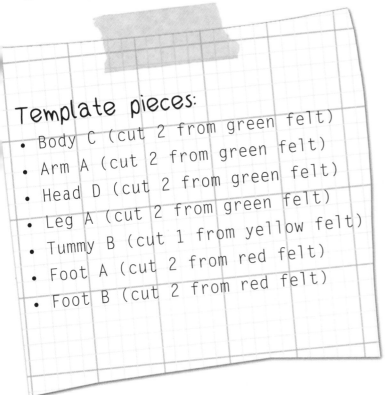

Template pieces:
- Body C (cut 2 from green felt)
- Arm A (cut 2 from green felt)
- Head D (cut 2 from green felt)
- Leg A (cut 2 from green felt)
- Tummy B (cut 1 from yellow felt)
- Foot A (cut 2 from red felt)
- Foot B (cut 2 from red felt)

This froggy is great for catching flies, but he's good at keeping secrets, too!

1 Glue the whole of the back piece of the head and add cotton wool or tiny felt scraps in the centre to make the head fatter. Stick the front piece on top and press around the edges firmly.

2 Glue the inner edge of the legs and stick them to the sides of one body piece. Glue feet A in place at the bottom of the legs.

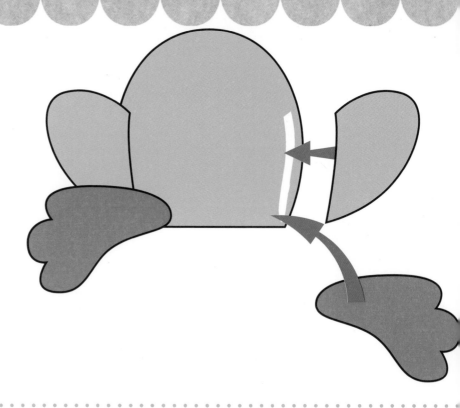

3 Turn the body over and glue carefully around all the edges, except the bottom. Stick the front body piece in place.

4 Glue the tummy piece in the middle of the body.

5 Dab a small amount of glue at the top of each foot B, and stick each one to the bottom of the tummy. The feet should flap freely at the front ends.

6 Glue each arm to the side of the tummy, using the bottom part to hold the feet B firmly in place.

7 Glue the head just above the tummy. Glue on the goggle eyes at the very top. Finish by drawing a big, wide-mouthed smile and two nostrils. Leave to dry overnight.

You will need
- 2 x goggle eyes
- A black fuzzy stick
- Glue
- Cotton wool or felt scraps
- Felt: black, white and red

Lucky Ladybird

Template pieces:
- Body C (cut 2 from black felt)
- Head C (cut 2 from black felt)
- Bug Wing (cut 2 from red felt)

Cut your own:
- Spot (cut 4 from black felt)
- Mouth (cut 1 from white felt)
- Antenna (cut 2 from red felt)
- Tummy (cut 1 from black felt)

Ladybirds can bring you luck. We've called ours 'bug' on the templates.

1 Ask an adult to cut the fuzzy stick into three equal lengths. Also ask them to bend the sharp ends over.

2 Carefully glue around the edge of a body piece and stick the other body piece on top. Press around the edges and leave to dry.

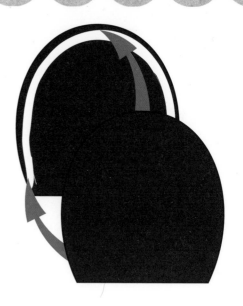

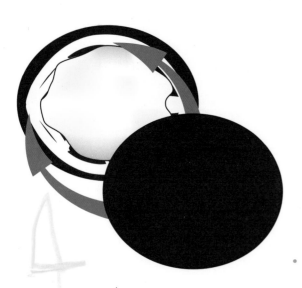

3 Glue one side of the bug's head and add cotton wool or tiny felt scraps in the centre to make the head fatter. Stick the other head piece over the top and press firmly all around the edges.

4 Glue the bottom of each antenna and stick in place at the top of the head piece.

5 Turn the head over and stick on the goggle eyes. Carefully glue the smiley mouth in place, then stick the head at the top of the body.

6 Turn the body over and glue on each wing. Leave a small space between the wings at the top. Glue the spots onto the wings.

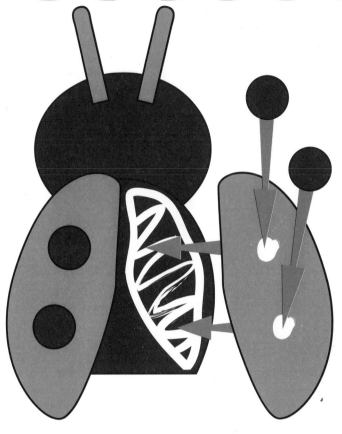

7 Turn the ladybird over again and carefully glue the legs across the body. Bend each leg into shape, then stick the tummy over the top of the legs, in the centre. Squash the puppet under a heavy book to dry overnight.

You will need
- 2 x goggle eyes
- A black pen
- Felt: white, black, yellow and orange
- Glue

Beady-eyed Toucan

Template pieces:
- Body A (cut 2 from black felt)
- Face (cut 2 from white felt)
- Wing D (cut 2 from black felt)
- Beak B (cut 2 from yellow felt)
- Beak C (cut 2 from orange felt)

Cut your own:
- Beak stripe (cut 2 from black felt)
- Eye (cut 2 from orange felt)

You too can make a toucan! It looks like he's keeping his eye on everything, so watch out!

1 Glue around the edges of the two beak B pieces and stick together. Now glue the top edge of beak B and stick it in place at the front of one body part, right at the top.

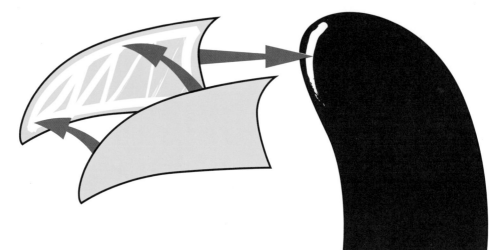

2 Carefully glue around the edge of this body part and beak, except the bottom edge, and place the other body section on top. Press firmly all around.

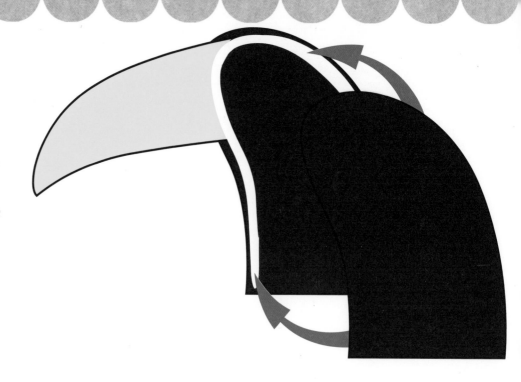

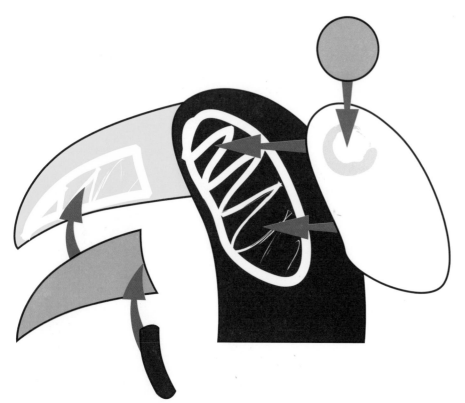

3 Glue a beak C piece in place on one side. Glue the beak decoration at the top edge, near the face. Turn the puppet over and do the same on the other side of the beak.

4 Glue a face piece in place on the body. Add the eye circle near the top. Turn the puppet over to glue the face and eye circle on the other side.

5 Glue one wing in place, just at the base of the face and across the bottom of the body. Turn the puppet over to glue the other wing in place.

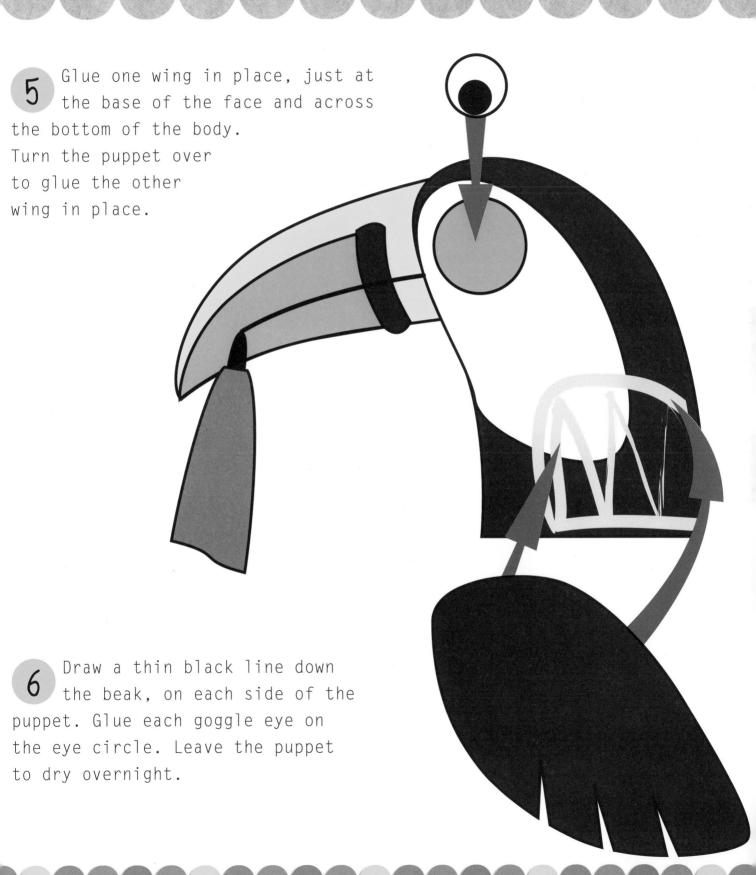

6 Draw a thin black line down the beak, on each side of the puppet. Glue each goggle eye on the eye circle. Leave the puppet to dry overnight.

You will need
- 2 x goggle eyes
- A black pen
- Cotton wool
- Glue
- Felt: grey, white, brown and pink

28

Bouncy Bunny

Template pieces:
- Body D (cut 2 from grey felt)
- Head E (cut 2 from grey felt)
- Cheeks A (cut 1 from white felt)
- Ear A (cut 2 from grey felt)
- Ear B (cut 2 from pink felt)
- Tummy C (cut 1 from white felt)
- Arm B (cut 2 from grey felt)

Cut your own:
- Nose (cut 1 from brown felt)
- Paw (cut 2 from white felt)

This cute, fluffy bunny is in a world of her own!

1 Glue one side of the rabbit's head and add cotton wool in the centre to make the head fatter. Stick the other head piece over the top and press firmly all around the edges.

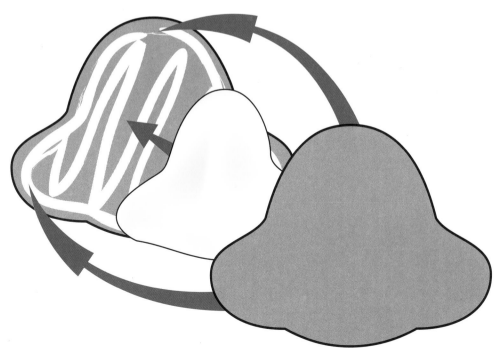

2 Glue the ear B pieces on top of the ear A pieces. Glue each completed ear behind the head, at the top.

3 Turn the head over and glue the cheek A piece across the front. Stick the nose in place.

4 Glue carefully around the edge of one body piece and place the arms near the top. Add more glue at the top of the arms and stick the front body piece on top.

5 Glue the paws in place at the ends of the arms.

6 Stick the tummy to the front of the body.

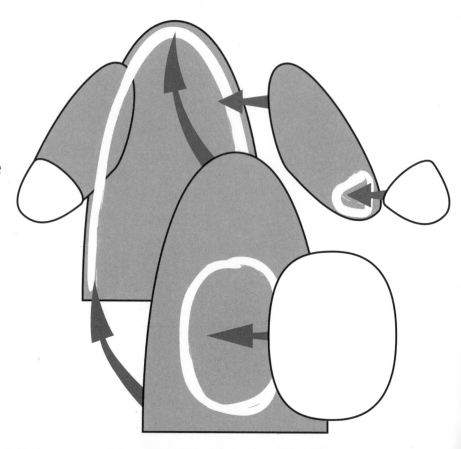

7 Glue on the goggle eyes and draw in a little mouth. Stick the head to the body.

8 Turn the rabbit over and glue on a small, fluffy cotton wool tail. Leave the puppet to dry overnight.

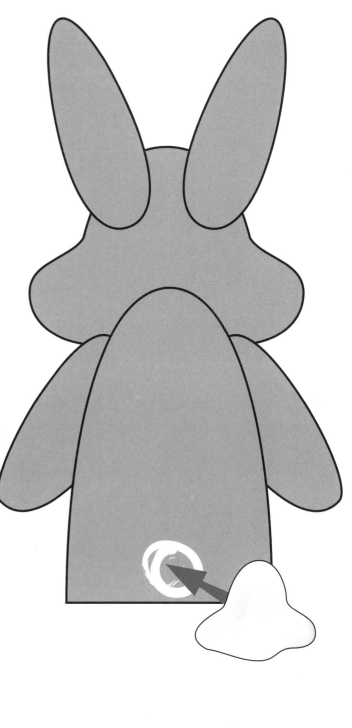

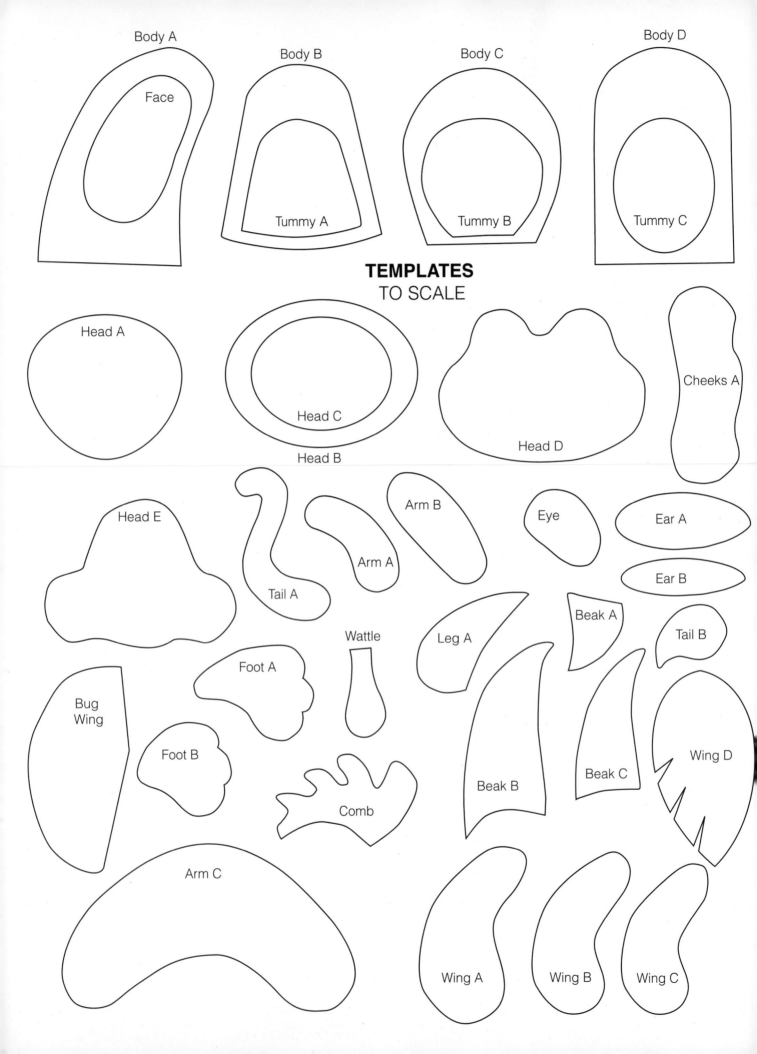

Body A

Face

Body B

Tummy A

Body C

Tummy B

Body D

Tummy C

TEMPLATES
TO SCALE

Head A

Head C

Head B

Head D

Cheeks A

Head E

Tail A

Arm A

Arm B

Eye

Ear A

Ear B

Beak A

Tail B

Wattle

Leg A

Bug
Wing

Foot A

Foot B

Comb

Beak B

Beak C

Wing D

Arm C

Wing A

Wing B

Wing C